To the memory of Eric Mort
in grateful thanks for his encoura
and enthusiasm

'FALMOUTH FOR INSTRUCTIONS'

THE STORY OF FALMOUTH IN
THE GREAT WAR, 1914 - 1919

JOHN POLLOCK

Published by J.B. Pollock, Penray, Perranwell Station,
Truro, Cornwall, TR3 7PF

Printed by Mid Cornwall Printing
Unit 5, Newham Industrial Estate, Truro TR1 2ST

PREFACE

This short account of Falmouth during the Great War is largely, but not exclusively, taken from the local press of the time, that is to say, *The Falmouth Packet* and *The West Briton.* Other sources are listed in the Bibliography.

I am very grateful to the staff of the Cornish Studies Centre, Redruth, for their unfailing courtesy and help. I am equally grateful to Mr. Peter Gilson for permitting me to examine the documents of the time held by the Royal Cornwall Polytechnic Society, Falmouth, and for allowing me to take copies of the Society's photographs relevant to that time.

In my footnotes, I have used initials to represent the following:

FP - *Falmouth Packet*
WB - *West Briton*
WMN - *Western Morning News*

CONTENTS

Page

'FALMOUTH FOR INSTRUCTIONS'

FALMOUTH IN THE FIRST WORLD WAR, 1914-1919

CHAPTER I

A CLOUD NO BIGGER THAN A MAN'S HAND
EARLY 1914

By 1914, Falmouth to a marked extent reflected the country as a whole - prosperous, deservedly self confident, already well established as a leading holiday resort, with plenty of hotels and guest houses to suit all pockets, and a port which, whilst no longer basking in the glory days of the packet ships, boasted one of the finest harbours in the world.

The borough had a population of 13,136, who, with their visitors, both holiday makers and seafarers, were served by 28 fully licensed public houses, 4 'beer licences' and 6 off licences, then known as 'grocers' licences'. Throughout the summer of 1913, Falmouth had enjoyed a record number of visitors, but, according to the Mayor, there was no drunkenness, which 'proved that those who came amongst them were of an exceptionally high character and, together with the inhabitants, were very abstemious'.[1] The number of cases of drunkenness recorded in 1913 was 32, all male, which was an increase of one on the figure for 1912, and, at a time when alcohol abuse was a major scourge, the Mayor had good reason for satisfaction with these figures.

The annual report of the Medical Officer of Health, Dr. A. Gregor, noted a steady improvement in the health of the borough,[2] but all was not sweetness and light. An enquiry had heard 'striking evidence... not only as to the wretched housing conditions in some parts of the borough, but of the difficulty experienced by labouring classes to get housing accommodation of any kind', and a small start to remedy this was the inauguration of a scheme for the erection of 44 'workmen's dwellings'. Some ruined buildings on Greenbank had been removed and replaced by a public garden, but on two other pressing problems, improved access to the borough and the installation of a system for sewage disposal, no progress had been made, and none was expected in 1914.[3] Dr. Gregor also complained in his report of 'the want of cleanliness in some houses... (and) there is still a lack of observance of the most elementary rules of hygiene'. He saw the need for public education in these matters, and proposed the holding of 'a health week in November... (which) ought to do an immense amount of good in bringing about a desire to live under better conditions, and in making the whole locality cleaner and more healthy'. Dr. Gregor was also concerned about the purity of the milk supplied to the borough, and called upon the East Kerrier Rural District Council to ensure 'rigid and systematic supervision of everything that concerns the dairy farming business in the rural districts'.[4] New soup kitchens, in which were installed two boilers of 80 and 60 gallons capacity respectively to hold the soup, were opened in Smithick Hill in February 1914 'for the supplying of cheap dinners to children and the working classes'.[5]

In 1914, Dracaena Avenue did not exist, and the main entrance to the town was along Greenbank and down High Street. As and when properties came on the market, the Corporation acquired them in order to widen High Street, which was very narrow and caused logjams for both motor and horse drawn vehicles, as well as dangers for pedestrians. The Corporation were anxious to acquire more properties which they thought 'would obviate the necessity of making a new approach to Falmouth'.[6]

A record number of in-patients, 97, had been treated at the hospital in 1913, and of which 85 had been surgical cases. The average number of in-patients on any one day was 7 and, again on average, there were 3 operations a week. In their report, the hospital committee pointed out that 'a very large proportion of patients came from Penryn and they feel that more support should be forthcoming from residents in that town'. The hospital, which was then at the top of Killigrew Street opposite the entrance to the Recreation Ground, was run on a financial shoestring, and the committee could not see their way to clearing the deficit of £24, 'without which they would be able to go forward with renewed vigour during the coming year'.[7]

At the quarterly meeting of the Falmouth Free Library, it was reported that during the past year 34,789 books had been issued. One of the committee, Mr. Webber, wondered whether the executive committee 'would take their courage into their hands, and weed out a lot of books in the library, which were rubbishy stuff'.[8] Unfortunately, he was not pressed on what he considered to be 'rubbishy stuff'.

By the early summer of 1914, it was clear that Falmouth could expect another record number of holiday makers, made possible by the fast and efficient railway service from London, the Midlands and the North. In addition, Falmouth had a growing reputation as an ideal place for convalescence and recuperation, and people in need of these would spend several months there. One such was a Mr. D.K. Glazer, who wrote to the *Packet* making some complaints concerning the lack of amusements for visitors in the winter. Starting with the closing of Gyllyngdune Gardens on a Sunday, he continued:

'There is nothing in this town during the winter but pictures. I am sure that if you had a good band once or twice a week, charge for chairs to sit around the grandstand like other seaside places, you would find it pay over and over again. Then, again, on a Sunday there is nothing. A sacred concert would be good for everyone either in the Pavilion or the grounds.... . A number of visitors I have met have said how deadly dull this place is, and would not return for this very reason, and they go on to Torquay or Ilfracombe. But you do not do anything until July. That is too late; we get nice weather in April. Falmouth is a lovely place, but it wants waking up and to cater for winter residents as well as July and August visitors. I am very glad to see that you have busses and charabancs. Well, they ought to run on Sundays. Other places do. Also allow small boats out. It would bring money into the town if there was more doing'.[9]

Sport in the town was not as healthy as one might expect in a thriving holiday resort. The rugby clubs of both Falmouth and Penryn had ceased to exist, a fact which the *Packet* deplored in a leading article, calling upon the Mayors of the United Borough to set up a meeting to lead to the formation of a joint club strong enough to take on all comers in the county.[10] At the annual general meeting of the Falmouth Golf Course Company, a deficit of £184 for the year was reported, and one of the directors, Mr. C.H. Hext, complained that whilst the importance of a well maintained golf course to a holiday resort was obvious to all, the townsfolk in general did not give it the support it deserved. It was, he said, 'a good deal more important than the building of a pavilion in any garden or the provision of any fresh gardens'.[11] A frequent visitor to Falmouth wrote from London to suggest that the Club would attract many more holiday makers if the green fee charged was reduced from an 'exorbitant' 2s 6d to 1s 6d.[12]

The cricket club was in a parlous financial state, and a loss for the year of £46-17-1 was reported at the annual general meeting. Amongst the expenses was a salary of £18 a season paid to the professional. On the field, the club was breaking even, with ten wins, ten losses and only one draw, which suggests that at least they were playing attractive cricket. However, the members were uncertain whether they could continue for another season as the debts mounted, one member asking 'whether it would not be better to face the fact that cricket is dead in Falmouth, and to do our best to pay off the debt'. Eventually, it was decided to continue the club for another year, on the understanding that if they could not pay their way then, it would have to be disbanded.[13] A small insight into the social caste system of the time is provided by a report in the *Packet* of a cricket match between Falmouth and Camborne. In listing the teams, six of the Falmouth X1 are given initials in front of their surnames, and five are not; none of the Camborne X1 are given initials. Whilst in first class cricket, the distinction between amateurs and professionals was shown by the former being given initials in press reports, it is known that Falmouth had only one professional, and Camborne would have had the same. The only conclusion to be drawn is that the newspaper awarded initials to those who it considered to be 'gentlemen', and not to those of an 'inferior' social class.[14]

The swimming club was flourishing with over one hundred members, but the only other sports which were in good heart were soccer and tennis. There was a Falmouth & District soccer league, which in April 1914 was headed, somewhat surprisingly, by St. Gluvias Debating Society, closely followed by Falmouth Rangers and Foudroyant.[15] The town boasted two tennis clubs, and again one senses a social distinction, with the 'toffs' at the Falmouth Club on Western Terrace, and the others at Falmouth Belmont Club. Both clubs were full, and visitors to the town could not get a game, so the Corporation was considering a plan to build public courts in Queen Mary Gardens. The *Packet* was not in favour of this, pointing out that the local MP had spent several hundreds of pounds of his own money on the gardens, and that there was not room for both tennis courts and gardens.[16] The Corporation decided not to proceed with the scheme, although years later the courts were built across the road from the gardens.

A tragedy occurred in February, when a German four masted barque, *Hera,* somewhat bizarrely mistook the St. Anthony light for the moon and went aground. The crew took to the lifeboat, but this overturned and nine managed to scramble back onto the wrecked vessel and clung to the mast, but by the time that the Falmouth lifeboat arrived, five of these had been swept away. In total, 19 out of a crew of 24 were lost.[17] The harbour was busy with the usual trading craft, and also more unusual visitors. Within a fortnight of each other, two liners, *Bassano* and *La Correntina,* came in with, in the one case, her cargo on fire and, in the other, 1,800 tons of coal on fire. It was no easy job to deal with these, because huge quantities of burning material had to be taken out of the holds and bunkers to get to the seat of the fires, and gangs of men worked in relays for several days to achieve this.[18] On another occasion a Norwegian four master was towed into the harbour with the captain already dead from beri-beri and seven members of the crew grievously ill. Dr. Lanyon, the port medical officer, described the sick men as 'the thinnest body of men I have ever seen'. The good doctor took a robust attitude to possible malingerers. One man complained that he could not feel his legs. 'Of course', said Dr. Lanyon, 'one does not always believe all that sailors tell one. To look at the man, there appeared to be nothing the matter with him, but I caught hold of a good bunch of hair on his leg by the roots and gave it a strong pull, keeping one eye on the man and the other eye on the leg, but the man did not make a sound'.[19]

The *Packet* printed each week a list of the ships which had come into the docks. In a typical week, that ending 20th. April, twenty vessels, including two naval ships, were in the docks, some discharging coal and loading china clay, some discharging maize and loading barley, and several simply described as 'trading.[20] The labour involved must have been immense; for instance, having unloaded a cargo of coal, the crew would then have to scrub clean the hold from any trace of coal dust before the china clay could be loaded.

Politically the United Borough of Falmouth and Penryn returned a Conservative, or Unionist, member of Parliament, Major C.S. Goldman, 'and so great a hold has he obtained on the esteem and affection of his constituents that the Liberals apparently consider their position as hopeless'.[21] 'Votes For Women' was a live issue in Falmouth, where there was a branch of the National Union of Women's Suffrage. A public meeting was held in April 1914, which was addressed by a Miss Muriel Mathers. The keynote of her speech was that women's suffrage was not simply about the right to vote, 'it was the demand for human rights for human beings, regardless of sex and irrespective of class'. She quoted, among much laughter, the late Mayor Gaynor of New York, 'if the British government would only provide British women with husbands, the movement would die down'. Miss Mathers said that the great protest marches in London gave the lie to this; the women of all classes who took part in these were looking for justice, not husbands. The resolution 'that this meeting demands a Government measure to enfranchise women' was passed unanimously.[22]

The *Packet* had no time for free trade, and held up Germany as an example to be followed of a nation which had achieved prosperity with the aid of tariff barriers. 'It is useless to talk of schemes for the uplifting of the masses so long as their wages are kept down to the barest minimum through the unrestricted competition of the foreigner in our home market'. Import duties on foreign goods would 'safeguard the home market from unfair foreign competition, provide more employment at better wages for our workers, and at the same time raise the revenue necessary to secure the future safety and well being of the whole body politic'.[23] The paper backed up this message with almost weekly cartoons, protesting against the 'dumping' here of foreign goods, and supporting protectionism. There is no doubt where the newspaper's political allegiance lay; in commenting on the latest budget, the *Packet* fulminated against the Liberal Chancellor, Lloyd George:

'Wherever he appears as a law giver, wasteful outlay, litigation, confusion and purposeless worry follow in his footsteps. His statutes are constructed with an eye to platform use and electioneering manoeuvres and are not devised with any genuine regard either for the facts or the interests to which the measures apply'.[24]

The lovely summer of 1914 blossomed. Great public interest was shown in the arrival in Falmouth of Sir Thomas Lipton's yacht, *Shamrock 1V,* en route for the USA to challenge for the America's Cup, a contest which was fated never to take place.[25] Two brothers, joint managers of the Star Theatre, 'a portable building now located in the Market House, Falmouth', were declared bankrupt, and the cause of their failure was attributed to 'the opening of picture palaces in several towns in

Cornwall visited by us, thereby causing a great reduction in takings at our theatre'.[26] The Kozey Cinema in High Street was doing good business, at 3d and 6d a seat; its choice of films was eclectic - in the week of the 26th. June there was a bill of 'Confederates in Crime', 'Jane Eyre' and 'Quicksands of Sin'.[27] The High School's production of Moliere's *Le Bourgeois Gentilhomme* was highly acclaimed; 'the proficiency of those who took part, alike as to their histrionic ability and the fluency with which they spoke the French dialogue, came as a revelation to many'.[28] It would be interesting to know how many in the audience understood that dialogue.

A tragedy was the suicide of the wife of the famous painter, Sir Alfred Munnings, by taking poison.[29] The Cornish Riviera Summer School for Arts and Crafts, using the High School and Clare Terrace and Wellington Terrace schools, was opened by the Mayor.[30] Visitors flooded into the town, the pleasure boats did a roaring trade, and the hotels and guesthouses had the 'no vacancy' signs up. The Falmouth Hotel Company, which owned the Bay and Pendennis Hotels as well as the Falmouth itself, reported a very satisfactory year and declared a dividend of ten per cent.[31] One of the pleasure boats, *The Queen of the Fal,* was instrumental in preventing a major disaster. Her captain noticed that, in foggy weather, a magnificent four master, the *Ben Lee,* was sailing directly onto the Manacles; he sounded his ship's siren frantically, which attracted the attention of some nearby fishing boats, and the fishermen immediately saw the danger. They went alongside the *Ben Lee,* boarded her, and she was brought round, 'her sides almost scraping the huge outer rocks'.[32] A French aviator caused great excitement when he landed his Bleriot monoplane on Gyllyngvase Beach, but, in so doing, disaster was only narrowly averted. The nose of the plane dipped into the sand and the plane came to a halt in a perpendicular position with its tail in the air, but Monsieur Selmet and his passenger escaped unhurt.[33] Selmet seemed to live a charmed life; very shortly after this episode, he was flying to Weston-super-Mare when his plane's engine failed, and he and his passenger 'were flung into the sea from a great height'. Surprisingly, neither was hurt, and they were rescued by a rowing boat.[34]

M. Hemel's plane 'lands' on Gyllyngvase Beach

The Falmouth Spring Flower Show was held in Gyllyngdune Gardens, and the local MP, C.S. Goldman, in his speech mentioned that there was a bill before Parliament to prohibit the use of birds' plumage in ladies' hats, and that it was his intention to propose the use of Cornish rhododendrons in its place.[35] If the Flower Show was mainly for the gentry, the Fair, held each year on the Moor in June, was definitely for the populace. The respectable element did not approve of the Fair. 'To huddle in a confined space such a conglomeration of exhibitions as occupied the Moor last week is courting grave danger to the town from disease'. Councillor Rickard also pontificated that Falmouth people could not spend so much on their pleasure, and also pay their debts.[36] A squadron of four battleships, under the command of Rear Admiral R.K. Arbuthnot, who was to lose his life at Jutland, visited the port in early June, and a ball and a cricket match were arranged to celebrate the occasion. The cricket match, between Falmouth Club and the Royal Naval side, aroused considerable interest as the Navy had the services of a nephew of the famous W.G. Grace, as well as of the gallant admiral himself. In the event Falmouth won easily, Grace's nephew and the admiral contributing 3 runs between them.[37]

Some things never change. The local Liberal candidate stated at a public meeting that 'this country is sick and tired of the Irish question'.[38] The *Packet,* having commented on the proposed change of the Royal Navy from coal to oil burning, went on, 'The matter is of course of even closer personal interest to thousands of motorists who have for some time past groaned impotently under the steadily increasing cost of petrol'.[39]

It was extremely unusual in the early 20th. century for anyone to reach the age of one hundred, and Falmouth was very proud of Mrs. Anne Bailey, who died in May 1914 at the age of 101. She had given an interview to a local journalist when she attained her century, in which she remembered Falmouth 'in the old smuggling days, when coffins filled with spirits used to be carried through the streets at night', to deceive the Revenue men. She described the town in those days as 'like a dungeon at night' because there was no street lighting, the first attempt at which were tallow candles. Mrs Bailey remembered the excited crowds at the harbour when the first steam ship arrived, and that fires were lit on the Beacon to guide ships into the harbour.[40]

NOTES

[1] The Mayor at the annual licensing sessions, FP, 6.2.1914, p8
[2] FP, 6.3.1914, p4
[3] FP, 2.1.1914, p2
[4] FP, 6.3.1914, p4
[5] FP, 20.2.1914, p6
[6] FP, 29.5.1914, p5
[7] FP, 13.2.1914, p7
[8] FP, 15.5.1914, p8
[9] FP, 26.6.1914, p8
[10] FP, 20.3.1914, p5
[11] FP, 6.2.1914, p3
[12] FP, 18.2.1914, p3
[13] FP, 1.5.1914, p7
[14] FP, 8.5.1914, p3
[15] FP, 3.4.1914, p6
[16] FP, 12.6.1914, p4
[17] FP, 6.2.1914, p7
[18] FP, 2.1.1914, p5
[19] FP, 16.1.1914, p8
[20] FP, 1.5.1914

[21] FP, 2.1.1914, p2
[22] FP, 3.4.1914, p5
[23] FP, 30.1.1914, p7
[24] FP, 6.3.1914, p4
[25] FP, 24.7.1914, p3
[26] FP, 22.5.1914, p8
[27] FP, 26.6.1914, p1
[28] FP, 22.5.1914, p3
[29] FP, 31.7.1914, p6
[30] FP, 31.7.1914, p6
[31] FP, 18.2.1914, p4
[32] FP, 8.5.1914, p4
[33] FP, 24.4.1914, p5
[34] FP, 8.5.1914, p3
[35] FP, 17.4.1914, p3
[36] FP, 26.6.1914, p4
[37] FP, 3.7.1914, p
[38] FP, 24.4.1914, p7
[39] FP, 24.4.1914, p4
[40] FP, 8.5.1914, p6

CHAPTER II

WAR!

Controversy rages to this day as to whether or not the declaration of war in August 1914 came as a shock. Clearly the ruling élite and the well educated upper middle classes were fully aware of the threat which Germany posed, but nevertheless it would appear that the vast majority of the public had little, if any, idea of the immediacy of that threat. Certainly the local Member of Parliament made no reference whatsoever to Germany in his speech at the annual meeting of the Penryn Conservative Club in March.[1] In February, the Mayor had presided over a public meeting to hear the views of the National Service League, which advocated compulsory military service. In his opening remarks the Mayor said that he wanted to hear both sides of the argument, and wished to be assured that if an army of a million young men was mustered it would be used for home defence and not for aggression. He was proud to be mayor of 'a town that had done more than its fair share in the Territorial movement and had sent many of its sons to the Royal Navy both on deck and below. They had also given a good many young men to the great mercantile marine, and any man who was in the English Channel on a night like this was doing a great national service'. Lt. W. Brockman RN put the case for compulsory military service, arguing that without it, and therefore an army to protect the home land, the regular army could not fight overseas. In his view, the Territorial Army was only partially trained and could not be expected to stand against regular troops. Mr. R.A. Sampson asked if he could give the opposing view, to which Lt. Brockman objected, saying that if Sampson wanted to oppose the ideas of the League he should call his own meeting. Sampson replied that 'that was hardly English, opportunities were generally given to persons holding contrary views'. Despite his opening remarks the Mayor then interjected 'it is hardly a debating society', but Brockman withdrew his objection and Sampson was allowed to speak - but not for long. Again the Mayor intervened, asking Sampson not to make a speech but to confine himself to questions to Brockman, so Sampson merely said that he was totally against the scheme, and a resolution was put supporting the League's demand for compulsory military service - which was lost by 19 votes to 18.[2] A meeting attracting less than 40 Falmouth inhabitants does not suggest a wide public debate, and the even split in the vote showed no overwhelming support for the ideas of the League.

What gripped the nation far more than the threat from Germany was the government proposal for Irish Home Rule, which already that summer had precipitated the Curragh mutiny. No less than 5,000 attended a demonstration at the Recreation Ground against Home Rule, addressed by Admiral Lord Beresford, and many more had been expected if it had not been for the heavy rain that evening.[3] Whilst there may have been no great enthusiasm for compulsory military service, the territorial army was active, and attracted a large number of young men by its social activities as well as the military. There were three companies in Falmouth, No.6 Company, Duke of Cornwall's Royal Garrison Artillery, Cornwall Fortress Royal Engineers, and 'C' Company, 4th Battalion Duke of Cornwall's Light Infantry, and in addition to a busy programme of drills, marches and practises, each ran a football team.[4]

It can safely be said that anyone who got their news of the outside world solely from the local press will have had no idea that Germany posed an immediate military threat, although there was concern over that country's multiplying merchant marine and the threat which that posed to Britain's domination of world trade. In May 1914, the *Packet,* in criticising the size of Lloyd George's budget, was able to assert that they were living 'in a period of profound peace'.[5] The assassination of the heir to the throne of the Austro-Hungarian empire, the Archduke Franz Ferdinand, and his wife, at Sarajevo was very briefly reported in the *West Briton* and slightly more fully in the *Packet,* which stated that 'the political consequences are likely to be grave', but the main impression of the report is one of sympathy for the aged Austrian Emperor, 'weighed down with years and broken by so many tragic sorrows'.[6] A review of the fleet at Spithead by the King, which was in effect a test mobilisation, was briefly reported; what astonishes the reader today is the colossal size of the fleet - 493 warships, totalling one million five hundred tons.[7] It is apparent that the focus of both papers was on the problems in Ireland, and nothing further on the mounting crisis across the Channel appeared in the *Briton* until the 30th July, when it was described as a European problem. Even as late as the 1st August the attitude of the *Briton* was that it was a very serious matter for continental powers, but there was no mention of possible British involvement. The *Packet* did explain to its readers on the 31st July that 'England may be involved if the war is not localised. Everything depends on the extent to which Russia will go to support Servia (*sic*)', because of the network of continental alliances which might, and in fact did, drag Britain into the conflict.[8] Even then, the threat of war only shared equal billing with the case of a dog which swam from Flushing to Falmouth without a collar, for which heinous offence the owner found himself in the magistrates' court.

As July slipped into August, troops began arriving in Falmouth by train, causing 'considerable consternation'. Civilians and tradesmen employed at Pendennis Castle had been given notice to leave, and sentries were guarding both Castle Drive and the Castle itself. One hundred men of the Irish Fusiliers were billeted at the castle and battalions of the DCLI were accommodated in sheds at the docks and at the Castle.

On the 4th August, war was declared against Germany and her allies. Under the heading, 'War!', the *Packet* expressed what was no doubt the universal feeling outside the political élite. 'England is at war with Germany. It was expected that it would happen some day, but few realised that it would come with such suddenness and be brought about by so remarkable a chain of circumstances'. Turning from the national and general to the local and specific, the *Packet* continued: 'Falmouth is now housing a population greatly in excess of its usual dimensions, and we would impress on the local public the desirability of assisting the sanitary authorities in keeping the town sweet and clean. All waste material should be burnt as far as possible, and refuse bins should be put out in good time to ensure prompt and regular collection. It is of the first importance that we maintain an unblemished bill of health'[9] The *Briton* stated that there was four months supply of food in the country, and that with the Navy protecting the trade routes, there was no fear of shortage, but that panic buying was already pushing up prices unnecessarily and there was a need for those at home to 'respond to the needs of the hour in a manner worthy of the splendid traditions of our Empire'.[10]

The sense of public shock at the outbreak of war was well expressed by *Punch.* 'Four weeks ago we stood on the verge of the great upheaval and knew it not. We were thinking of holidays; of cricket and golf and bathing, and then were suddenly plunged in the deep waters of the greatest of all wars. It has been a month of rude awakening, of revelation, of discovery - of many moods varying from confidence to deep misgiving'.[11]

But what did 'War' mean to the average Falmouthian? Some fourteen years before, a volunteer army had sailed to the Cape of Good Hope to fight the Boers, and forty five years before that an army had fought in the Crimea, but there had been no large scale conflict for a hundred years involving British fighting men on the continent. Wars were something which happened a long way away, and did not greatly affect the average citizen, unless he or she had a relative in the armed forces - and in any case Britain was always the winner. The fact that the enemy would have to be fought across the Channel brought the conflict nearer to home, but 'over by Christmas' was the prevalent and confident attitude, and the invincible British navy made any idea of invasion quite laughable. Many young men rushed to join up, fearing that 'all the fun' would be over before they could get into battle, whilst the older generation would have frowned at the dislocation of business and trade and the tiresome regulations which war always brings. No one, from the King downwards, had any idea of what was before them, and the outbreak of war was probably more of a nuisance than a horror for nearly everyone enjoying high summer in Falmouth.

The Bishop of Truro's message to his Cornish flock, on the outbreak of war, was 'To pray devoutly, and hammer away stoutly'.[12]

NOTES

[1] FP, 13.2.1914, p5
[2] FP, 13.2.1914, p5
[3] FP, 26.6.1914, p7
[4] FP, 6.2.1914, p8
[5] FP, 15.5.1914, p2
[6] FP, 8.7.1914, p2

[7] FP, 17.7.1914, p2
[8] FP, 31.7.1914, p3
[9] FP, 7.8.1914, p4
[10] WB, 6.8.1914, p4
[11] *Mr. Punch's History of the Great War*, p1
[12] Bob Dunstan, *The Book of Falmouth and Penryn*, 1975, p108

CHAPTER III

THE DARK HORIZON

The declaration of war had four immediate practical effects in the borough, a considerable influx of soldiers, a huge increase of shipping in the harbour, the requisitioning of horses for war purposes, and panic buying of food.

All members of the Territorial Army were immediately called up, and the Princess Pavilion was commandeered by the Army for billeting troops at a rent of £20 a week.[1] In addition to Falmouth, troops were stationed at St. Anthony, and one soldier there 'received a bayonet thrust and is in a very critical condition. The wound is stated to be received during a quarrel which took place in the village of Gerrans'.[2] Discipline at St. Anthony seems to have been on the lax side as there were five cases in a week of soldiers from there being absent without leave, causing the Mayor to remark 'that he could not understand young men who were patriotic enough to join the Army giving so much trouble afterwards'.[3] As the war went on, and a large camp was built at Trevethan, local people got used to the town being thronged with soldiers, but at first there were problems caused by the influx of a large number of young men. Apart from cases of drunkenness, which were dealt with to some extent by closing the public houses at 9.30pm, more serious offences were committed, such as the conviction of a Royal Fusilier for enticing a 9 year old girl into a quarry and committing 'a common assault', for which he was fined ten shillings with costs of 12s 6d.[4] An offence which frequently came before the bench was the harbouring of soldiers absent without leave. The first offender of this nature was one Elizabeth Uren, of Webber Street, who was let off with a caution, but the magistrates made it known that 'future offenders would be dealt with most severely'.[5] They were as good as their word, as when a woman was similarly charged of harbouring her cousin, she was sent to prison for four months with hard labour.[6] It seems that her excuse that she thought that her cousin had been discharged from the Army with varicose veins did not satisfy the court. Yet another deserter was found in bed with the woman who had harboured him. In this case, the legal reason for the case coming before the court hardly figured in the report. What really shocked the *Packet* was that the couple had been caught in *flagrante delicto,* and the headline read, 'Terrible Story of Depravity'.[7]

All the local schools were taken over for use as military hospitals, but one Royal Fusilier was unfortunate enough to injure his toe and was taken to hospital to have his toe nail removed under anaesthetic, 'a slight quantity of chloroform', but this induced a fatal heart attack.[8] The Polytechnic Hall was opened for use by soldiers, 'magazines, newspapers, games, stationery etc. are provided free, and teas are also supplied at cheap rates'.[9] A new territorial company was formed immediately on the outbreak of war, the Electric Light Company, Royal Engineers, whose task it was to service the electric communications within the port, the lighting of the borough and the mobilisation of the defences.

When war was declared, two large German liners of the Hamburg-Amerika line, *Kronprinzessin Cecilie* and *Prinz Adalbert,* were in Falmouth harbour and were promptly arrested, and men of the 4th Battalion Duke of Cornwall's Light Infantry were placed on board, not without difficulty as the crews refused to handle the ropes of the tug or do anything without the instructions of their owners.[10] There was no question of the ships making a dash for it, as two cruisers, *Endymion* and *Theseus*, were guarding the entrance to the harbour. It was thought that the *Kronprinzessin Cecilie* was carrying a large quantity of bullion, but a thorough search of the vessel proved that this was not the case, and the two cruisers were released to join their squadron.[11] However, it was feared one night that the German liners were trying to escape, as a gun was fired in the harbour. It transpired that a coasting steamer had neglected to stop at the entrance to the harbour, and a warning shot was fired across her bows. When the authorities boarded the steamer, they found the captain 'in a fright', as he had been told that he could enter Falmouth without any restriction.[12]

The passengers from the liners, many of them German, were taken ashore and accommodated in various Workhouses, from Penzance to St. Columb, and Falmouth took 108 of these.[13] The crews were not made prisoners of war on 'giving their parole of honour', and the Board of Guardians were faced with the task of feeding and looking after nearly 400 persons, many of whom were free to roam the streets of the town. The expense of this task caused the Guardians to postpone a scheme for heating water in the Workhouse,[14] and the Corporation and Board of Guardians jointly petitioned the Government to set up a concentration camp for these aliens, possibly on Bodmin Moor, without success. In asking for help with the expense, the Corporation pointed out that 'inasmuch as the nation has taken, and will reap the benefit of the captured German steamers, the nation should therefore bear the cost and expense incurred or to be incurred by the local authorities at once, and that the same be made a national charge'.[15]

A fortnight later, two American heavy cruisers, *Tennessee* and *North Carolina,* came into Falmouth carrying several million dollars in gold for the relief of Americans stranded in Europe, as a result of the outbreak of war.[16] This money was transferred under heavily armed guard by train to the

USS Heavy cruiser 'North Carolina' at Falmouth, August 1914

USS Heavy cruiser 'Tennessee' at Falmouth, August 1914

American cruisers and captured German ships in Falmouth, August 1914

American Embassy in London. A British cruiser, the *Talbot,* intercepted the 12,500 ton liner *Potsdam,* and diverted her to Falmouth. On board were 400 German reservists returning from America, and these were taken from the ship and made prisoners of war and taken to Dorchester by special train. 'The visitors were a most respectable looking lot of men, many being first and second class passengers'.[17] In early September, five German ships were captured and escorted into Falmouth. These were a four masted barque, with a cargo of timber, a steamer of 2,476 tons and a crew of 24, *Orlando,* 2065 tons, with a cargo of nitrate, a motor auxiliary schooner with a cargo of wood, and the aptly named *Fritz,* 2000 tons, with a cargo of nitrate.[18]

A resident of Falmouth, Mrs. Faith Harris, kept a diary throughout the first three years of the war of the comings and goings of ships to and from the harbour, and, in addition to the various enemy prizes, she tells us that the harbour in those early days was packed with ships of every size and nationality, which had come in to get instructions how to proceed in the changed circumstances. During September a powerful squadron of four battleships and three cruisers were stationed in the Bay, and they brought into the port several prizes including a Dutch liner with Austrian reservists on board. However, an example of the inevitable confusion which war brought in the very early days was the interception of a Norwegian sailing ship by the cruiser, *Endymion.* She was carrying a cargo of salted hides bound for Hamburg, and had previously been directed into Falmouth. There, instead of the cargo being confiscated, for some reason she was given clearance by Customs officials, and proceeded on her way. When stopped by the *Endymion,* the captain produced the certificate of clearance from Falmouth, and for the second time she was allowed to proceed unmolested to Hamburg.[19] Rear Admiral de Chair, in reporting the incident to the Admiralty, stated 'I consider that the action of the Falmouth officials would appear to assist the enemy. It is not understood how they could have let her proceed as the most casual examination must have raised their suspicions'.[20]

One of the first changes which the residents of Falmouth would have noticed was the complete absence of horse drawn cabs, as horses were immediately requisitioned by the Army. In those days of great reliance on horse power, this requisitioning caused considerable difficulties. 'In some cases, a man was deprived of the only horse he possessed, whilst five out of seven animals belonging to one firm were commandeered'. A party of 56 from the Breage Wesleyan Band of Hope were on an outing to Falmouth in horse drawn vehicles, but on nearing the town the drivers heard of the commandeering of horses and refused to go any further, so their passengers had to walk the rest of the way.[21] All excursions aboard the *Princess Victoria, Queen of the Fal* and similar pleasure steamers were cancelled, and tugs were requisitioned for war work. Nervous sentries were involved in two shooting incidents; a foreigner, believed to be German, was shot in the leg in High Street, and a Redruth man, returning home in his pony and trap with his two sisters after a visit to Falmouth, was challenged by a sentry on North Parade; thinking it was a joke, he continued on his way, only to be shot, again in the leg, but not seriously injured.[22]

With the declaration of war, the immediate reaction was for people to stock up their larders. This resulted in shortages and rising prices, and 'a feeling in the town that an attempt was being made to corner articles of food with the object of making money out of the poor'. In a couple of days the price of sugar had gone up from 15s per hundredweight to 45s. There was disagreement among the members of the Corporation as to whether or not local traders were 'hoarding', but a resolution warning against it was carried.[23] A government notice appeared in the *Packet,* surrounded by a heavy black border, reading: 'Every member of the public who discovers that any tradesman is charging increased prices for food is requested by the Government to forward his name and address to the Commercial Department, Board of Trade Offices, Whitehall'.[24]

The *Packet* immediately issued advice for the civilian population. 'The primary duty of every housewife is to prevent waste... Puddings that require flour should give place to milk puddings, stewed fruit and simple savouries. Every effort should be made to save fuel. Bread should not be served when fresh, but be kept until stale, when it will be more digestible and less wasteful, and every scrap can be utilised for nursery puddings... Vegetables dressed in different ways are an excellent resource and very good for the health'. Under the heading 'Rules for Men', the *Packet* advised that 'the forgotten art of walking is a fruitful way of economy', particularly of fuel. Men should also resolve:
      'To work in the garden instead of golfing,
      Not to smoke a cigar,
      To see to it that any stores of food you have are not damaged by mice
      000or that your fruit is protected from the birds.
      To save a gallon of petrol
      To do small repairs yourself'[25]

In October, the town held a Belgian Day, on which artificial flowers in Belgian colours were sold at a penny or tuppence each in aid of destitute Belgian refugees in this country, 'the victims of the Prussian bully's blood lust'.[26] The local bench had to deal with a case of incitement to mutiny on an American hospital ship in the harbour. A waiter on the ship was assaulted by another member of the crew, following which at an angry meeting of the waiter's colleagues, the defendant threatened to fling overboard the Master-at-Arms, and incited the rest to defy the latter's orders. The case was dismissed on the defendant agreeing to return to his ship 'and conduct himself in a proper manner'.[27]

The population had no doubt braced themselves for a nasty shock in Lloyd George's November budget, and they got it with income tax being doubled - to 1s 6d in the pound. Duties on beer and tea were also increased. The Government decided in November that a war widow should receive a pension of 7s 6d per week, plus 5s for the first child, 2s 6d for each of the second, third and fourth children, and 2s for any subsequent child.[28]

Three weeks after the outbreak of war, the *Briton* reported that 'the war has seriously affected the many people of Falmouth who mainly derive their livelihood from the several ways in which visitors are catered for at the sea resort'. The town was empty of visitors, but their loss had been offset to some extent for the hotels and boarding houses by the number of liners forced to put into Falmouth, which in normal circumstances would not have called there, and from which 'large numbers of passengers were accommodated in the town for varying periods'. Trades people too had been able to offset part of the loss due to the absence of holiday makers by supplying the increasing number of troops arriving in the town. Again, in the docks there was no increase in unemployment, as the absence of china clay shipments had been offset by the unloading of ships captured on their way to enemy ports. There was a shortage of labour at the foundry, as over one hundred of the work force of between 400 and 500 had joined the armed forces. The *Western Morning News,* under the heading '1914 in Falmouth', asserted that 'but for the war, nothing of note would have been available for record', since the town had continued on its quiet way, administering to a large number of holiday makers. Whilst these ceased with the outbreak of war, they were replaced by so many soldiers 'that instead of losing by the absence of ordinary visitors, the town has gained to a very large extent. Many thousands of military have undergone training here, and at times the normal male population has been more than doubled. Pendennis Castle has been filled to its fullest capacity, a number of hutments have been erected in various places in and around Falmouth, the Princess Pavilion has been occupied, and numerous large houses have been secured for the accommodation of troops. At St. Anthony, too, on the other side of the harbour, a large number of troops have been quartered, so that altogether the town has had a busy time'.[29] Further proof of the unexpected benefits which war could bring was the installation in November 1914 of a mail and passenger steamship service between Falmouth and Bilbao, to take the place of the pre-war Southampton-Bilbao service which had been closed down because of the danger from submarine attack to ships proceeding up the Channel. Believing in striking whilst the iron was hot, the Chamber of Commerce wrote to the Spanish Prime Minister requesting that the change from Southampton to Falmouth be made permanent.[30] War also brought a bonanza for the port's pilots, with the vastly increased shipping calling at Falmouth, although once a boom defence was constructed from St. Anthony to Porthallow, pilots were not allowed to operate outside the harbour limits.[31]

The current number of the *Medical Press & Circular* contained a similar upbeat assessment of Falmouth's position, taken from a different angle: 'The Corporation of Falmouth have sent us the official guide to that town and its environs, thereby hoping that the publication of a clear and illustrated statement of its claims as a winter health resort may attract some of the throngs of pleasure seekers, and of delicate individuals who yearly migrate to the French, Italian and Algerian coasts from the United Kingdom on the approach of winter. That Falmouth has justification for its claim of '*Queen of the West*' on the Cornish Riviera must be admitted by all who have personal knowledge of the beauties of nature here revealed; and the tables of sunshine furnished by the medical officer of health tend to prove that visitors will not miss much in this direction through enforced absence from their accustomed Continental residences... The army of invalids will naturally seek advice of the medical profession, and they will moreover have this item to the credit of their purse, and of fatigue, that through the enterprise of the Great Western Railway Company they have now but six hours' railway journey from London, in luxurious trains to reach that beauty spot, Falmouth, on the Cornish Riviera'.[32]

Turkey had come into the war on the side of Germany. Canon Hitchens of St. Georges Cathedral, Jerusalem, wrote to his parents, who lived at Pennance House, Falmouth, that the Turkish authorities had confused ecclesiastical canons with military cannons. A Turkish officer and a detachment of soldiers entered the cathedral to search for the supposedly hidden 'cannons', removing the altar and the floor beneath. Whilst the soldiers were carrying out their search, the officer first sat on the Bishop's throne and then 'played a selection of operatic airs on the harmonium, until reproved by Canon Hitchens for levity'. Having found no cannons, the officer contented himself by alarming Canon Hitchens with the hope that 'the church would shortly be filled with the blood of the congregation', and then took his leave.[33]

The *Briton* contained a graphic description of the fraternisation between the British and the German forces which took place in the trenches on Christmas Day, 1914. It seems to have started with the Germans erecting on their parapets on Christmas Eve trees decorated with candles, the firing stopped and both sides sang carols. Some German officers then started to walk across No Man's Land and were met in the middle by their British counterparts, where they exchanged cigarettes and souvenirs. This encouraged the mass of the soldiers to swarm out of their trenches and meet in the middle - 'we took them out some tea and cocoa, which they eagerly accepted'. Whether the famous football match took place seems open to doubt; a man in the Rifle Brigade wrote to his parents, 'we also agreed to play a football match with them on Christmas Day, and we got a ball ready, but their colonel would not allow them to play, so we had a game on our own. It seemed a treat to get a bit of exercise, and in the evening we entertained each other with sing-songs until about 10.00pm, and that ended our Christmas of 1914, which was very enjoyable under the circumstances. Just after midnight, you could hear, away on the right, the plonk-plonk of bullets as they hit the ground, and we knew the game had started again'.[34]

NOTES

[1] FP, 18.9.1914, p6
[2] FP, 2.10.1914, p4
[3] FP, 16.10.1914, p4
[4] FP, 13.11.1914, p4
[5] FP, 30.10.1914, p4
[6] FP, 26.3.1914, p4
[7] FP, 4.6.1914, p2
[8] FP, 6.11.1914, p4
[9] FP, 16.10.1914, p4
[10] WB, 10.8.1914, p2
[11] Rear Admiral de Chair to the Admiralty, 27.8.1914,
    The Maritime Blockade of Germany in the Great War,
    J.D. Grainger, editor, Navy Records Society, 2003, p27
[12] FP, 7.8.1914, p4
[13] FP, 14.8.1914, p8
[14] FP, 7.8.1914, p8
[15] FP, 14.8.1914, p6
[16] FP, 6.11.1914, p4
[17] FP, 6.11.1914, p4
[16] FP, 21.8.1914, p4
[17] FP, 28.8.1914, p4
[18] FP, 11.9.1919
[19] Navy Records Society, ibid., p39
[20] Navy Records Society, ibid., p106
[21] FP, 7.8.1914, p5
[22] FP, 11.9.1914, p4
[23] FP, 7.8.1914, p5
[24] FP, 7.8.1914, p3
[25] FP, 7.8.1914, p2
[26] FP, 20.10.1914, p3
[27] FP, 2.10.1914, p4
[28] E. Sylvia Pankhurst, *The Home Front*, p81
[29] WMN, reprinted in FP, 8.1.1915, p3
[30] WB, 5.11.1914, p2
[31] FP, 28.2.1936, retirement of Capt. Bickford, pilot p4
[32] Medical Press & Circular, reprinted in FP, 6.11.1914, p6
[33] FP, 8.1.1915, p3
[34] WB, 4.1.1915, p3

CHAPTER IV

SPY MANIA

The fear and hatred of Germans in the early days of the war were fanned by reports of atrocities committed in Belgium. A private in the DCLI wrote to his parents in Falmouth that his cousin had told him that 'he (the cousin) was one of a body that arrested ten Uhlans, and in the pocket of one, they found a girl's hand. Needless to say, he was taken out and shot immediately... That sort of thing ought to encourage young men to enlist, for what would happen to their mothers, sisters and sweethearts if the Uhlans came to England?'[1]   So often, as in this case, these reports were second hand, but few cared about their veracity. Members of the establishment were not slow in pouring petrol on the flames; Lord Harewood pronounced that: 'All Germans should be expelled at once. They ought to have been expelled within 48 hours of the declaration of war... As for naturalised Germans, I do not believe in them at all. If the Government will not help us, then we must help ourselves, and I should not scruple, if I had a weapon and I found anyone I suspected to be a German engaged in a suspicious operation, as the Americans say, 'to shoot on sight''.[2]

It is hardly surprising that the result was a paranoia about German spies, from which Falmouth suffered in full measure. It seems that anyone with a camera or a 'strange' accent, such as a Londoner, was liable to instant arrest and to be transported to Falmouth police station, where he was interrogated by Superintendent Nicholls - and then released. The *Packet* reported that 'All sorts of rumours have been circulated during the week as to the presence of spies in the town, and their arrest. Perhaps the fact that a large number of foreigners, including the crews from the German liners, were walking aimlessly around the town, gave rise to the many tales that have been told'.[3]

Many examples of spy mania appeared in the local press.

A well known ships' chandler, Johannes Engel, of the Quay, was arrested on suspicion of having committed an offence under the Official Secrets Act, and remanded in custody for eight days. He had once been in the German Navy. No evidence was offered, and the Bench was asked for his release; he would be served with a deportation order, re-arrested and sent to Bodmin Prison. As he left court, there was an affecting scene between Engel and his wife, and cries of 'Judas' and 'Traitor'. A young man, B.C. Lowry, of Smithick Hill, dashed through the crowd and seized Engel by his long beard, both falling to the ground. Engel was driven off in a taxi, amid jeers, to Penryn; Lowry was taken to the police station, followed by the cheering crowd, but later released without charge.[4] Engel had been a well known and respected figure in Falmouth commercial life for many years. His sons had grown up in Falmouth, one served his apprenticeship with Messrs. Cox and Co., at the Foundry, and was at the time of his father's arrest an artificer in the Royal Navy, while another son was in the Royal Canadian Mounted Police.[5]

A student of geology in the Perranwell area with a map and German textbook was suspected of 'tapping telephone wires', but was found to be a respectable London schoolmaster on holiday. On being taken to Falmouth police station, 'he was badly mobbed, and a portion of his coat was torn away. Women shouted all kinds of nasty expressions at him, and he was struck on the side of the face. On reaching the police station he was soon able to prove his innocence to the police and he was released. Mr. Upton returned to London with his family on Monday, and he will not soon forget his experience at Falmouth last Friday'.[6]

A Danish national living at Budock was arrested 'on the groundless charge of signalling from Budock Downs to passing ships', and then released. He received a written apology from the parents of the girl who gave the 'information' to the military authorities.[7] A printer from Torquay on holiday in Falmouth, returning on the steamer from St. Mawes, 'asked some questions regarding the garrison'. He was arrested on suspicion of being a spy, and taken to the police station, interviewed by Supt. Nicholls and released.[8] A local tailor was charged with 'being in the vicinity of military works in possession of a camera' whilst walking on Gyllyngvase beach. The magistrates dismissed the case because he had acted unwittingly, but made him pay the costs of 6s 6d.

'The lookout at St. Anthony had seen someone signalling to a Dutch liner, brought up in the outer Roads, on which there were some German reservists. Part of the message was in the usual Morse code, which was read, but part was in Dutch. Whereupon a squad of twelve men was sent across to investigate matters and surprise the enemy. Needless to say, with no result, for the spy had decamped... There are many Dutch vessels in the roadstead, and Germans are resident on both sides of Falmouth harbour... The country is riddled with spies; yet the unsuspicious take no positive measures to cope with the danger'.[9]

A prominent Truro jeweller, Mr. J. Pearson, was forced to put a notice in the *Briton* week after week to the effect that the rumour that he was of German stock was untrue. The same paper described as 'unfounded' a rumour that the ex-county surveyor, Mr. A.E. Brooks, had been arrested as a spy in Durham.[10]

An artist, Rolph Jonsson, who was a Swedish national and had been for some years a member of the Newlyn School and a pupil of Stanhope Forbes, was tried by court martial in Falmouth accused of signalling to enemy shipping. Jonsson, or influential friends, were able to engage the services of the famous KC, Marshall Hall, who secured an acquittal on all counts.[11]

The hostility to aliens extended to those lodged at the Workhouse. Ten of these, 'all above middle age', were brought before the magistrates accused of 'refusing to turn over certain ground, the task allotted to them'. All ten pleaded physical ailments and disabilities, which prevented them from doing the heavy work. The interpreter engaged by the court was apparently unable to translate the oath, 'shall be the truth, the whole truth and nothing but the truth... amid laughter Major Mead (one of the magistrates) remarked that there was evidently no place for it in the German language'. The accused were all convicted of being 'incorrigibly lazy', and were sent to prison for 21 days with hard labour.[12] The Guardians decided that the enemy aliens in the Workhouse must be fed margarine, for fear that the townsfolk would withhold their rates if they knew that these inmates were eating butter.[13]

One of the most unfortunate victims of this fear and hatred of aliens was an elderly cattle dealer, Frederick Moeller, who had lived and worked in this country for 39 years. He had been born a Dane, in a province of Denmark which later was annexed by Prussia in the war of 1866, and thus against his will he became a German citizen. As such, he had to do two years compulsory service in the German army, after which he escaped to England, and never again visited Germany. When war broke out, Moeller immediately applied for British nationality, but his application had not been dealt with by the time that he landed in Falmouth after a business trip to Buenos Aires in January 1915. He was arrested and brought before the local bench, charged with being an enemy alien who had landed in this country without permission, and was fined £50.[14]

In the febrile atmosphere then persisting, it is somewhat surprising that Mrs. Faith Harris felt able to keep her detailed record of the comings and goings of shipping in the harbour, especially as a retired sea captain taking his daily walk, stopped to look at the harbour through his telescope - and was promptly arrested.[15]

NOTES

[1] FP, 20.11.1914, p2
[2] FP, 18.9.1914, p2
[3] FP, 14.8.1914, p4
[4] FP, 14.8.1914, p4
[5] FP, 7.8.1914, p5
[6] FP, 14.8.1914, p4
[7] FP, 2.10.1914, p4
[8] FP, 28.10.1914, p4

[9] FP, 9.10.1914, p4
[10] WB, 22.10.1914, p3
[11] WB, 4.3.1915, p3
[12] FP, 28.10.1914, p6
[13] FP, 2.10.1914, p6
[14] FP, 1.1.1915, p2
[15] FP, 15.1.1915, p4

CHAPTER V

KEEPING THE HOME FIRES BURNING - 1915

As 1914 merged into 1915, the early optimism of a quick victory faded, although the *Briton,* in less than certain terms, ventured 'it is surely not unreasonable to believe that Germany cannot hold out for a further twelve months'.[1] By May, however, the paper was counselling its readers to 'abandon hope of a partial collapse of the German forces' and that 'the war is likely to continue for many months longer'.[2] The residents of Falmouth gradually settled down for the long haul.

In January 1915, an order was issued by the Garrison Commander that no lights visible from the sea were to be shown. All street lights 'with the exception of those in the main streets' were extinguished and 'the town was plunged into darkness'. Evensong at All Saints was brought forward to 3.30pm, so as not to breach 'the blackout'.[3] However, the *Briton* reported that of 344 lamps in the town, 106 were still lit.[4] 'A prominent resident' was summonsed for breaching black out regulations. As this was the first case, the bench decided that a warning, plus costs of 10/6, was sufficient but that 'any future offenders would be severely dealt with'.[5] The darkening of the town, which as has been seen was not a total black-out, continued to be a bone of contention. At a meeting of the Corporation, Mr. Spargo said that 'It seemed strange to him that certain parts should be in darkness, and yet the main street was so brilliantly lighted, especially on a Saturday night. Supposing an aircraft visited the locality, it would have no difficulty in locating the principal part of the town and where the gas works were situated. It seemed somewhat ludicrous to ask that some parts of the town should be darkened and others were kept lighted'. He received the abrupt reply from the Mayor, 'there is a very good reason' without further exposition of that reason.[6] The times for 'obscuring lights' were printed in the *Packet* each week. It seems that certain of the townsfolk at least were never reconciled to these lighting restrictions; as late as November 1917, letters were still being written to the *Packet* complaining that 'the lighting restrictions of Falmouth are ridiculous and very dangerous to pedestrians'.[7]

Instructions were issued to the public as to the steps to be taken if Falmouth was shelled by a German battleship, or bombed by enemy aircraft. These included turning off all gas and electrical appliances, extinguishing all fires and oil lamps, staying indoors, avoiding crowding together, and taking shelter in the nearest cellar.[8]

It seems that even the criminal element began to mend their ways in time of war. Mr. Justice Scrutton at Cornwall Assizes said that 'the wave of law abidingness and good behaviour, which at this time of national emergency has swept over the kingdom, had, of course, not left unaffected the loyal county of Cornwall'. Sadly, that did not save a 51 year old woman, suffering from mental disorder, from a sentence of two months imprisonment for attempting to commit suicide.[9]

The question of recruitment for the armed forces will be dealt with in the next chapter, but appeals for volunteers shed light on the class system of the day. One such appeal read, 'A Question For You to Answer. Have you a butler, groom, chauffeur, gardener or gamekeeper serving you who at this minute should be serving his King and Country?'[10] Similar pressure was put on employers further down the social ladder:

'The War - 4 Questions to Employers:
1   Have you given every fit man under your control every opportunity of enlisting?
2   Have you encouraged your men to enlist by offering to keep their positions open?
3   Have you offered to help them in any other way if they will serve their country?
4   Have you any men still in your employ who ought to enlist?'[11]

As the summer approached, and just to prove that it is an ill wind, it was hoped that Falmouth might attract visitors who would normally go abroad in peace time or to east coast resorts, which were now threatened with bombing. Hotels in the town were well booked, but not so the cheaper guesthouses, and this was accounted for by the absence of pre-war railway cheap excursion tickets, the cost of travel being a big factor for many.[12] The war brought new business opportunities, amongst which were tenders invited for contracts for 'barrack services' for the Army, 'comprising sweeping chimneys, purchase of old straw, removal of ashes and rubbish, deodorising and emptying of privies and closets and cleansing of latrine strainers'.[13] The port also derived benefit from the war. Liners to and from New York, the West Indies and South America continued to call at Falmouth, not only to embark and disembark passengers but also to carry hundreds of bags of mail. Possibly the largest ship to visit the port was the Holland-Amerika line *Nieu Amsterdam,* 'one of the finest steamers engaged in the Atlantic passenger trade and has accommodation for 3000 persons'.[14] In August 1915, a new service was introduced with liners calling at Falmouth to embark passengers for New York, this being initiated by the *Nieu Amsterdam.*[15] In addition to liners, large cargo steamers called at Falmouth, including 'Dutch, Norwegian and Swedish steamers (with) their respective flags and names and ports of registry painted on their sides'.[16]

In those days of unmetalled roads, dust was a great problem. The state of Commercial Road, Penryn, was such that a councillor, Mr. Crothers, remarked that 'on Sunday when people went to church in nice black clothes, they must have looked like millers before they got there owing to the dust clouds'. The contractor employed to clear the dust heaps said that all his horses save one had been commandeered for the Army, but he was hopeful of getting a second shortly.[17] Mr. Crothers was the headmaster of the local school, and his son, in the Merchant Navy, had the dubious distinction of being torpedoed three times, surviving them all despite an inability to swim. After one sinking, he was landed in Falmouth and walked to Penryn still in his oil and water stained boiler suit, arriving home to the shock of his parents, who had no idea that his ship had been torpedoed.[18] A person under the pseudonym of 'Choked With Dust' wrote to the *Packet* complaining that 'the streets and roads of Falmouth since the dry weather set in are a disgrace to any decent town, due to not enough watering, resulting in clouds of dust'.[19] Falmouth and Penryn might form 'the United Borough' politically, but ancient rivalries still flourished. In looking for economies, Penryn Town Council considered disbanding its fire brigade, and relying on that of Falmouth. This aroused the ire of some members and a Mr. Sara commented, 'I think that it would be a slur on the town to be without a brigade. I am a strong supporter of keeping away from Falmouth as far as we possibly can'.[20]

From the outbreak of war, soldiers in ever greater numbers flooded into the town, both to provide a garrison, as Falmouth was considered of vital strategic importance, and also as a training area. The presence of the military will be dealt with in a later chapter, but at any one time upwards of 14,000 soldiers were stationed in the borough or just outside, and the schools at Clare Terrace, Wellington Terrace and Wodehouse Terrace, and also the Pendennis Hotel were taken over as military hospitals. The children ousted from the schools were divided, the boys going to the Friends' School Room, and also the reading room of the public library, the girls to Pike's Hill Sunday School and the infants to Earl's Retreat. It is perhaps hardly surprising that school attendance was stated to be 'at the lowest point in the records' of Falmouth District Education Committee, due to epidemics and children being kept from school to help on farms and in businesses.[21] In September 1915, the new building to house the Grammar School was informally opened by Sir Arthur Quiller-Couch, as it was felt inappropriate to have a formal opening in time of war.[22] By the end of 1915, these military hospitals and the Sailor's Home were looking after hundreds of sick and wounded men. For some reason, the Fortress Commander at Falmouth had decreed that Truro was 'out of bounds' to all troops, and it took all the persuasive abilities of the Mayor of Truro to get him to rescind this order; the Mayor pointed out that there were many Truro men either stationed, or in hospital, in Falmouth and that it was extremely unfair to prevent them from visiting their homes in Truro.[23]

The Mayoress launched an appeal for sandbags for the front line, at 6d each, stating that each sandbag 'will stop a bullet and probably save a soldier's life'.[24] 11,000 bags had been sent by the middle of August 1915. She then turned her attention to 'thirst quenching tins of fruit' to be sent to the troops fighting in the heat of the Dardenelles, and in September 1915, 984 tins of peaches, apricots and pineapples were sent.[25] Other people sent pasties to soldiers at the front; a soldier wrote that they made 'a fine picnic', seated with his 'chum in the trenches'.[26] Others tried to help British prisoners of war. Miss E. Byrne put a notice in the *Packet* to the effect that she was 'in constant communication with wounded and needy British prisoners of war, and would be glad to receive old or new clothing, also any oddments of wool with which to make comforts for these men, who are in dire need of such help'.[27] Queen Mary had set the pace with these appeals, and all the items which were sent to the troops in her name had a card attached to them, on which was written, 'From Mary and the women of the Empire'. This gave rise to the story that an officer, on receiving such a parcel and reading the card, looked puzzled, scratched his head, and was heard to remark, 'Well that's funny; I know all the women at the Empire, but I'm damned if I can remember which Mary is'.[28]

It seems that not everyone was so public spirited. A letter from 'Justice' complained of 'what is not only a grave injustice, but what is tantamount to a national scandal'. This related to Falmouth house owners or tenants 'charging extortionate prices to officers' for rooms. An example given was of an officer and his wife being charged 28s a week 'and extra for every scuttle of coal' for two rooms in an artisan's dwelling', and then being given one week's notice to vacate. 'There is no need for the Huns to come to England: they are here in spirit in the guise of people who, taking advantage of the death struggle of our nation, seek to batten upon the blood of our officers, who are dying for their country, in order that these human harpies may rest in contentment at home'.[29]

The residents of the borough had to accept many changes and restrictions, as the months went by. In addition to the population being doubled by the influx of soldiers, Castle Drive being closed, and the restrictions on lighting in the town, the military authorities stopped all harbour traffic between sunset and sunrise, causing inconvenience to local businesses.[30] Under the Defence of the Realm Act, fishing boats had to be licensed, and could then go to sea day or night, but, if at night, could not be within 10 miles of the entrance to a defended harbour, such as Falmouth, on pain of a fine of £100 and six months imprisonment.[31] Parliament then introduced the Light On Vehicles Order, which required every motor or horse drawn vehicle, trap or handcart to have front and rear lights for use after sunset. The object was that these lights would take the place of street lights and thereby make it more difficult for German bombers to find the towns. Blinds had to be pulled down in trains at night 'and the guard runs through the train to see that the order is obeyed'. But it was pointed out that railway stations were exempt from the Order, so that the whole exercise was made rather pointless by the huge lamps at Falmouth station, so conspicuous from every direction.[32]

Another burden for the residents to bear was the deterioration in the postal service. Many employees of the Post Office had volunteered for the armed forces, and applications by women to take their places had been held up by Post Office bureaucracy. The influx of army and naval personnel had added to the strain on the postal system, and the shortage of staff resulted in a bringing forward of closing time at post offices from 9.00pm to 8.00pm. The Chamber of Commerce complained of the chaos experienced at the head post office, due both to lack of counter space and the lack of 'division into compartments so that the public might know where to go to transact the different classes of business'. The Chamber also 'expressed the hope that the inconvenience caused by the alterations in the hours of collection and the delays in deliveries would be speedily ended'.[33] Recruitment for the forces also had a serious effect both on shops and on trains. The shortage of men meant that shops had to close for an hour at lunch time to give those who were left a break, and train services were curtailed. Those used to summoning a porter to carry their luggage found that they had to carry their own, and there was a proposal that passengers should take with them only the amount of luggage which they could conveniently carry themselves, although it is uncertain how far this was enforced.[34] An appeal was made to 'ladies who shop', to carry their purchases home themselves, 'or bring someone with them to do so', as there were no longer enough errand boys for every shop to deliver small packages.[35] Even the local newspaper, the *Packet,* was subject to press censorship, and various editions appeared with blank spaces marked 'Deleted By The Press Censor'.[36]

Another aspect of life which was concerning the Chamber of Commerce was the taxation of 'excessive war profits'. Whilst acknowledging that this was aimed at manufacturers and traders, members thought that the legislation should also cover the professions. Mr. H.H. Cox asserted that, 'the thing has been framed by lawyers who had kept themselves out. Professional men, such as lawyers and doctors, should be included'.[37] Whilst this seems fair, Mr. Cox did not explain by what methods lawyers and doctors were going to make 'excessive war profits'.

Overshadowing these comparatively minor irritations was the steady stream of deaths of servicemen from Falmouth reported each week in the *Packet,* often with photos, not only on the Western Front but in the Navy, at the Dardenelles, and South West Africa where R. Eathorne, for many years Cornwall's rugby full back and a sporting legend in the county, lost his life.[38] Mr. H.L.Williams, who lived at Greenbank, was the chief engineer on a liner, converted into the auxiliary cruiser *Bayano.* His wife had been up to Scotland to see him, but on the very day of her return to Falmouth, she received a telegram telling her of his death in the sinking of the ship by a torpedo off the Wigtown coast.[39] In August 1915, the troop transport, *Royal Edward,* was sunk in the Aegean, with between 20 and 30 believed to be on board from Falmouth. The *Packet's* headline read, 'Terrible Anxiety in Falmouth and District. Wives' Awful Suspense'.[40] Twelve of the men from Falmouth were saved, but fifteen were among the 1,011 lost in the disaster.[41] Private Herbert Truscott, on returning home to Falmouth, told the *Packet* of his ordeal. He saw the torpedo coming towards the ship, which was struck just under where he was standing:

'I felt that I had lost all sense of recollection for a moment or so; then I was lifted off my feet twice and thrown on my knees, whilst the water splashed about me. The transport began to founder and on looking round I saw one of my mates, to whom I spoke. He never replied, but simply looked at me, and I never saw the poor fellow again, for he was drowned. Fortunately I recovered my senses and had the presence of mind to take off my tunic and boots. I then lowered myself over the liner's side with a rope, but as fast as I was going down the *Royal Edward* was sinking with me. I climbed up the rope again and rested my foot on the transport's top rail. Then I felt that the suction was dragging me under. I threw myself off the rail and into the sea, and after swimming about a hundred yards managed to grasp some wreckage. Then I heard a terrible explosion, for the steamer's boilers must have blown up, and on looking around all I could see was the sky and the open sea. For three hours I clung to the piece of wreckage, but I was becoming so exhausted that I felt that I must soon let go. Eventually a boat from a hospital ship came along, rescued me and took me to Alexandria. I met several of my Falmouth chums on the hospital ship, and we were all most anxious to know what had become of our other comrades'.[42]

In the main, relatives heard of the fate of their loved ones not by telegram but by a buff-coloured envelope, with OHMS printed on it, which was delivered by the postman with the rest of the mail. The letter inside commenced with, 'It is my painful duty to inform you that a report has been received from the War Office notifying the death of...'.[43] One can only imagine the emotions of those finding such an envelope amongst the normal routine of bills, bank statements and even, in some cases, the last letter written from the front of the man to whom the buff envelope referred.

Many young Falmouth men were serving in the Royal Navy, in the Grand Fleet based at Scapa Flow which was carrying out the thankless but essential task of enforcing the blockade against Germany in the North Sea. One such, Fred Martin, wrote to his parents about the Navy's work:

'I can tell you that it is very hard to keep going up and down night and day in all weathers waiting for them, but it is like a cat watching a mouse... People are asking 'what are the Navy doing?' I can tell them that we are going through something up here that they don't know about, and we are keeping the dear old flag flying over them whilst they are asleep. It makes my blood boil to think that we can't get at them (the German fleet) properly and do a good job to them, and if people only knew what we are going through while the dirty dogs are in harbour safe at anchor, and we out steaming all the time, they would have some sympathy for the brave men of our British Navy. Then perhaps they would not keep saying, what are the Navy doing?'[44]

As dislike of the Germans hardened into hatred, two Swiss waiters employed at a Falmouth hotel were foolish enough as to display their German sympathies, as they were reported to the police as having 'rejoiced' at the sinking of the famous Cunarder, *Lusitania,* by a U-boat. They got short shrift from Superintendent Nicholls who ordered them to leave Falmouth within two hours, having first informed him of their destination.[45] The lengths to which prominent citizens sitting on the bench would allow their prejudices to go was illustrated by the case of the licence at the Ship and Castle Hotel, St. Mawes. The licensee, being a German subject, had been interned. Application was made for a transfer of the licence to Mrs. Howes, the English mother of the wife of the licensee, and letters 'from prominent persons who had been staying at the hotel in support of the application' were produced. The bench 'were unanimous in refusing the application, as they could have nothing to do with anyone having any connection with a German'. Application was then made for a transfer of the licence to the manager of the St. Austell Brewery, but this was refused also as the unfortunate Mrs. Howes would be in charge under the manager. A temporary transfer to the manager was granted 'on the understanding that another person would be put in charge of the house within one month'.[46] In addition to those with German connections, the Bench let it be known that 'they would look with disfavour on applications for transfer to men of military age'.[47]

The Anti-German League was formed in 1915. Its members undertook:
a   not to buy German goods after the war
b   not to employ German staff after the war
c   not to place contracts with German companies
d   to boycott any English trader stocking German goods when equivalent British goods were available.

The formation of a coalition government in June 1915 was welcomed by the *Packet,* claiming that 'the new Government commands the support of an undivided people throughout the United Kingdom... Of the few malcontents and sedition mongers in Ireland and Britain who are doing what they can to strengthen the hands of the Kaiser and the Prussian militarists and to promote the success of the new barbarism in its war against Christendom we may happily say that they are harmful only in intention'. Asserting that the nation 'had put away its political dissensions', it could now concentrate on saving 'our race from enslavement, our homes from the abominations that have made Belgium a land of martyrdom, and our religion from the ascendancy of the idolatory of brute force' and in this struggle the *Packet* expresses the faith which the nation had in Lord Kitchener, the War Minister, to bring in 'the measures which in his judgment are best for the Army at each succeeding stage of the struggle'.[48] Restating its satisfaction with the formation of a coalition government, the *Packet* declared that 'the front Government bench of the House of Commons now presents the appearance of a 'happy family'. The Liberal Lion shows no disposition to devour the Conservative lamb, the Free Trade fox has apparently no designs upon his Tariff Reform neighbour's hen roosts, and the Ulster watch dog blinks complacently by the side of the Home Rule cat. The Government is no longer of one party. It represents the nation'. The *Packet* went on to congratulate the Cabinet in 'having got rid of its Jonah - Lord Haldane', who was hated on the right for being thought, entirely unfairly, to be pro-German.

In June 1915, an Open Air Club was inaugurated on the Grammar School's playing fields, the objects of the club being 'to provide wholesome recreation in the way of organised games etc. for people over 14 years of age'. The club was aimed at both sexes and particularly at the troops quartered in Falmouth, and each member would pay a subscription of one penny a week. It was intended to provide cricket, badminton, croquet and other games, and also refreshments.[49] In September, a swimming gala was held on Gyllyngvase beach to raise funds for the War Hospitals Supply Depot. This was a very big affair, with some thousands of spectators, and grandstands being erected to accommodate them. The main event was a race from St. Anthony to Gyllyngvase, and 70 wounded soldiers from the local hospitals were entertained to tea. In the evening there was a public concert in the Pavilion.[50]

Somewhat surprisingly, the greatly increased numbers in the town did not result in extra business for the Falmouth Free Library. The executive committee reported 'a great falling off in the number of readers of books'. One member queried the expenditure of £10 on new books, 'he did not wish to be stingy, but it was a question whether new books were absolutely necessary'.[51]

Dr. Blamey, Medical Officer of Health for East Kerrier RDC, adjacent to the borough, was worried that children were not being vaccinated against smallpox in sufficient numbers, despite the united view of the medical profession that this was essential, otherwise there was the fear that smallpox would prove 'as powerful an enemy as the Germans'.[52] Dr. Gregor, MOH for Falmouth, reported that 'during the year 1914, the town has been as healthy as in normal years', and considered as 'very satisfactory' eleven deaths from tuberculosis, and 17 cases of infant mortality.[53] The war produced a variety of jobs for the able bodied, and by late 1915 it was said that of the 87 inmates in the Falmouth Workhouse, only two were fit to scrub, and none were suitable to look after the 14 children, five of whom were under three years of age. The officer in charge of children had resigned, and a question of job demarcation arose. The Board of Guardians were of the opinion that the workhouse was over staffed, and some members wanted to direct one of the officers to take charge of the children, but it was pointed out that each officer under his or her contract was employed to perform certain tasks and that it would be difficult to require an officer to perform additional duties.

Gyllyugvase Beach, Swimming Gala Day, 8th September 1915

Nurses and helpers at Gyllyugvase Beach,
Swimming Gala Day, 8th September 1915

A member of the Board, Mr. Andrew, disagreed - 'he thought that they had the right to tell the officers what they must do, and if they did not like it they could resign. It was not a question of their telling the Board what they were going to do'. He added that in his opinion all the officers had 'soft jobs', but his robust attitude was not shared by the Board as a whole.[54]

A tremendous gale hit Falmouth on 13th November 1915. 'The wind began to blow with hurricane force from the south east, and gradually it veered round to the north west. Seas like mountains rolled down Carrick Roads, and even in the inner harbour many vessels felt the strain... Many quay punts broke from their moorings and went ashore or fouled other craft, whilst scores of small rowing boats foundered at their moorings. On shore hundreds of roofs of houses were damaged and nearly every street was littered with slates. Huge trees were torn out of the ground at Arwenack Avenue,

'Implacable' launched in 1789 and fought at Trafalgar under French colours as the 'Duguay Trouin', used as a holiday ship for boys. Brought by G. E. Wheatley Cobb to Falmouth in 1912

'Implacable' returning to Falmouth Harbour after refit in Plymouth, having been towed down.

Grove Hill and Woodlane... It is reported that 100 trees were blown down at Carclew and 170 at Pengreep, the road at the latter place becoming impassable for some time'. The most dramatic incident of this storm involved the old sailing battleship, *Implacable,* then used as a training ship, anchored off St. Just-in-Roseland. It seems that there was one seaman and two boys on board that night. Seaman Foulkes told the story of their ordeal:

'It was the worst night I have ever experienced, and I have never seen any seas like those which prevailed on Friday night. They were quite 80 or 100 feet high and the wind was awful. You can imagine the force when I tell you it lifted a skylight, weighing over 8 hundred weight, off the deck of our ship and smashed it in pieces'. Worse was to come, as Foulkes saw a small schooner drifting down on the *Implacable,* and the inevitable collision caused considerable damage to the *Implacable's* side. Foulkes saw that the schooner would certainly run ashore and that in those seas the crew of three had no chance, so he threw a line aboard and the schooner was made fast to the *Implacable.* The schooner's crew, fearing that their ship would break up as she crashed against the training ship's side, made a jump for it and each was caught in turn by Foulkes. Only when safely aboard did Foulkes learn from the schooner's captain that there were 50 tons of cartridges and powder on the schooner. 'You can just imagine the awful sensation we all experienced. Every time the schooner crashed against the side of the three-decker and we felt the concussion, we wondered if we should be blown up'. Foulkes ordered the two boys to go to the forward part of the ship, as he feared that the stern would be blown off if there was an explosion, and they had to endure several more hours of the schooner crashing against the side of the old battleship, before the wind moderated, and a tug could get a line aboard the schooner and tow her to a safe anchorage.[55]

Despite the war, shipping was still a profitable business. 'Shares in the steamships under the management of Mr. R.B. Chellew were especially sought after and realised record prices. The Chellew fleet are at present paying excellent dividends and making exceptional returns to the shareholders'.[56] The fishing industry was also prospering. 'The fishermen of St. Ives are meeting with unprecedented success in the prosecution of the herring fishery', landing over 1 1/4 million herring in one day at a value of £4000.[57]

After one year of the war, Falmouth was a strategic port, a naval base and a training ground for thousands of troops, but it still managed to fulfill its peacetime function as a holiday resort. An article appeared in the *Daily Mail* under the heading of 'Glorious Falmouth'. It described how a family of four had come to Falmouth for their holiday for the seventh year in succession. One reason for their love of Falmouth was its informality - 'you don't have to spend a lot of money on promenading clothes here, or on doing what everyone else does... Whatever you may have a fancy for - sailing, swimming, fishing, boating, bathing or walking - is there to be done. You can spend as much money as you can afford or you can have the cheapest holiday in all England, and enjoy yourself thoroughly'. The author of the article, C.E. Hands, then launches into an astonishing one sentence, 170 word description of a ferry crossing from Falmouth to St. Mawes:
'This little family at a total cost for the four of two shillings had taken return tickets in the little pleasure steamer which plies across the vast expanse of the land-locked harbour among the anchored ships of the inner haven round Trefusis Point on the farther side, where the woods come down to the water's edge, across the mouth of the wide Carrick Roads, the estuary within the harbour into which the beautiful River Fal flows, and within which the big steamers and the tall four-masted sailing ships from the far seas are anchored, and there, looking out on the bay through the open sea gate, of which the gaunt, castle crowned headland of Pendennis on the one side and St. Anthony's craggy rocks on the other form the gateposts, makes for another point of jutting rocks upon which another

ancient castle stands sentinel, and rounding this comes into another little bay within the folds of the harbour, where there is the port and haven of St. Mawes'.

On and on in this purple prose floats Mr. Hands, but amongst all the hyperbole he does make the point that the war 'has restored to Falmouth a glimpse of its old importance and activity', with the harbour once more crowded with shipping. Also, he points out, there are really two Falmouths, the old town and the harbour being one and the new hotels overlooking the bay, well laid out gardens, tennis courts, and bathing beaches being the other - 'a very elegant and complete watering place indeed'.[58]

The Rector of Falmouth, the Reverend H.H. King, had had to go to Tenerife for the sake of his health. But his need for peace and quiet was rudely shattered, when he learnt how the Spanish authorities dealt with strikes. In his Christmas letter to the Mayor, he gave the following graphic description:
'It is said that an attempt was made to blow up an English steamer, whose cargo was being handled by 'blacklegs', with dynamite, and this was detected and frustrated by a Spanish gunboat in harbour. Whereupon the Military Governor at once dominated the situation. The town was put under martial law. Cavalry paraded the streets. All the principal buildings and offices were guarded by soldiers. The squares and streets were thronged with soldiers with loaded carbines and large drawn flat swords. The unfortunate strikers were harried over the hills and mountains. 500 were locked up in two days in forts and prisons, and the strike was broken! The soldiers were turned into the bakers' shops and baked all the bread necessary for the populace. It seems a drastic and high handed way of ending a strike, but I dare say that it was needed with an excitable race like the Spaniards, and it probably saved a good deal of bloodshed... But imagine similar methods applied to an English strike, say in south Wales!'[59]

By the end of 1915, there was no sign of a resolution to the debate over when the war would end - 'the prophecies vary from three months to three years, according to the weather and the disposition of the prophet. Meet a naturally cheerful man on a fine day, and he will persuade you that we are very near the end, and that the London gas fitter who said he was engaged in making decorations for the peace celebrations is one of the wisest of men'. On the other hand, there were those who could see no end to the conflict, but the *Briton* concluded that 'the cheerful men and women are more helpful than the gloomy ones, provided that while they are prepared for peace, they push forward the war work in every possible way'.[60]

NOTES

[1] WB, 11.1.1915, p2
[2] WB, 3.5.1915, p2
[3] FP, 22.1.1915, p4
[4] WB, 11.2.1915, p5
[5] FP, 19.2.1915, p4
[6] FP, 12.2.1915, p6
[7] FP, 16.11.1917, p3
[8] FP, 22.1.1915
[9] FP, 29.1.1915, p5
[10] FP, 12.2.1915, p2
[11] FP, 1.1.1915, p2
[12] WB, 10.5.1915, p2
[13] FP, 17.9.1915, p4

[14] FP, 23.6.1915, p3
[15] FP, 30.7.1915, p4
[16] FP, 26.2.1915, p3
[17] WB, 13.5.1915, p2
[18] Mrs. M. Tourell-Harris, Mr. Crothers' granddaughter, to the author
[19] FP, 11.6.1915, p6
[20] FP, 10.9.1915 p6
[21] FP, 2.4.1915, p4
[22] FP, 24.9.1915, p6
[23] WB, 15.5.1916, p2
[24] FP, 30.7.1915, p4
[25] FP, 17.9.1915, p4

[26] FP, 17.9.1915, p4

[27] FP, 3.12.1915, p3

[28] *The Bickersteth Diaries, 1914-1918, p15*

[29] FP, 12.3.1915, p3

[30] FP, 26.3.1915, p4

[31] FP, 23.7.1915, p4

[32] WB, 17.1.1915, p2

[33] WB, 10.6.1915, p8

[34] WB, 20.12.1915, p2

[35] FP, 23.7.1915, p4

[36] FP, 5.11.1915, p4

[37] FP, 8.10.1915, p4

[38] FP, 28.5.1915, p2

[39] FP, 19.3.1915, p4

[40] FP, 20.8.1915, p3

[41] FP, 3.9.1915, p4

[42] FP, 3.12.1915, p3

[43] Richard van Emden & Steve Humphries, *All Quiet On The Home Front*, p90

[44] Letter from Fred Martin to his parents who lived at Middle Terrace, FP, 29.1.1915, p4

[45] FP, 14.5.1915

[46] FP, 5.3.1915, p5

[47] FP, 1.10.1915, p4

[48] FP, 4.6.1915, p3

[49] WB, 21.6.1915, p2

[50] FP, 10.9.1915

[51] FP, 30.7.1915, p2

[52] FP, 13.8.1915, p2

[53] FP, 13.8.1915, p5

[54] WB, 4.10.1915

[55] FP, 19.11.1915, p6

[56] FP, 3.12.1915, p4

[57] FP, 17.12.1915, p4

[58] Daily Mail, 22.9.1915, as reprinted in the FP, 24.9.1915, p5

[59] FP, 13.12.1915, p6

[60] WB, 20.12.1915, p2

CHAPTER VI

'YOUR COUNTRY NEEDS YOU!'

In August 1914, Britain's armed forces were recruited entirely on a voluntary basis, and such was the deep rooted distrust of conscription and the idea of a large standing army, that it was not until two years into the greatest war the world had ever seen that men were obliged to join the forces by means of conscription. In January 1915, the *Briton* reported figures for recruiting produced by the six western counties. In a six week period a total of 4876 men volunteered, of which over half were rejected as being unfit for military service - a telling statistic indeed on the physical state of the nation.[1] In February 1915, 990 out of a total population of 17,115 in Falmouth and Penryn were serving in the armed forces, a percentage of 5.02, which was higher than any other parliamentary division in Cornwall other than South East Cornwall.[2] Despite this, there was anxiety as to 'whether Falmouth is doing its duty'. A local worthy and recruiting officer, Major Mead, speaking at a joint meeting of the local political parties to encourage enlisting, stated that, 'they had men in the town at present who had no right to be there. If they realised the position this country is in, and what they owed to their country, they had no business to be at home today'.[3]

From the outset of the war, there was anxiety over the failure, as it was perceived, of Cornishmen to rush to the colours. In reporting that the DCLI were to carry out recruiting marches in the county, the *Briton* commented 'efforts are being made to stir the young men of Cornwall to join the Army, but those who are actively engaged in the work are not sanguine of its results... . Here the men are difficult to move. Many listen to impassioned appeals with apparent indifference. Only very few are ready at once to decide to join the forces who are doing their utmost to crush the enemy'. The paper put down this indifference to a feeling that this was not 'their' war, and that it all seemed remote as they did not see, as other parts of the country did, 'the frequent arrivals of contingents of badly injured men, whose sufferings forcibly appeal to all who see them', or 'the departures of regiments of fresh troops leaving to take their part in the grim conflict'.[4] It appears that sons of farmers received a particularly bad press in this regard - 'all the recruiting returns support the statement that the farming section of the community has not contributed its fair proportion of young men'. The *Briton* then poses the question, if the young men are to be taken from the farms into the services, how are the farmers to respond to the call to make Britain as self sufficient in food as possible? The answer as suggested by the editor was to employ female and child labour, the latter being given special permission to leave school at the age of 12 to work on the farms.[5]

Unease was felt at the contrast of the horrors of death and maiming in the trenches, and the continuing amusements at home. 'Newspapers record horse racing to the extent of two or three columns and the illustrated papers give pages to depicting scenes that are devoted to pleasure - frivolous and giddy pleasure at the best... It indicates an insensibility to the terrible nature of the struggle and to the sacrifices that are being made by the men in the trenches... The truth is that we are not as a nation entirely intent upon the war. There are still a number of people who do not understand that the circumstances of life here in England have wholly changed. A rude awakening may come for them before they are many months older'.[6]

A four day recruiting march in late March 1915 from Falmouth to Helston and Redruth produced 72 recruits, 33 of which came from Redruth.[7] This was considered a very poor return, and the *Packet*

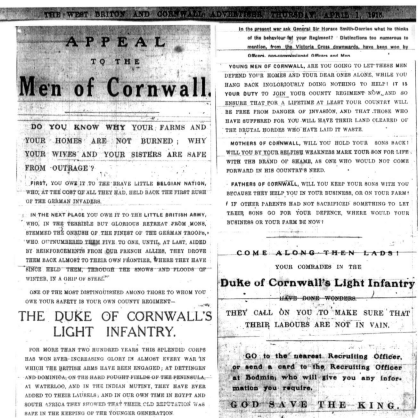

APPEAL

TO THE

Men of Cornwall.

DO YOU KNOW WHY YOUR FARMS AND YOUR HOMES ARE NOT BURNED ; WHY YOUR WIVES AND YOUR SISTERS ARE SAFE FROM OUTRAGE ?

FIRST, YOU OWE IT TO THE BRAVE LITTLE BELGIAN NATION, WHO, AT THE COST OF ALL THEY HAD, HELD BACK THE FIRST RUSH OF THE GERMAN INVADERS.

IN THE NEXT PLACE YOU OWE IT TO THE LITTLE BRITISH ARMY, WHO, IN THE TERRIBLE BUT GLORIOUS RETREAT FROM MONS, STEMMED THE ONRUSH OF THE FINEST OF THE GERMAN TROOPS, WHO OUTNUMBERED THEM FIVE TO ONE, UNTIL, AT LAST, AIDED BY REINFORCEMENTS FROM OUR FRENCH ALLIES, THEY DROVE THEM BACK ALMOST TO THEIR OWN FRONTIER, WHERE THEY HAVE SINCE HELD THEM, THROUGH THE SNOWS AND FLOODS OF WINTER, IN A GRIP OF STEEL.

ONE OF THE MOST DISTINGUISHED AMONG THOSE TO WHOM YOU OWE YOUR SAFETY IS YOUR OWN COUNTY REGIMENT—

THE DUKE OF CORNWALL'S LIGHT INFANTRY.

FOR MORE THAN TWO HUNDRED YEARS THIS SPLENDID CORPS HAS WON EVER-INCREASING GLORY IN ALMOST EVERY WAR IN WHICH THE BRITISH ARMS HAVE BEEN ENGAGED; AT DETTINGEN AND DOMINICA; ON THE HARD FOUGHT FIELDS OF THE PENINSULA, AT WATERLOO, AND IN THE INDIAN MUTINY, THEY HAVE EVER ADDED TO THEIR LAURELS; AND IN OUR OWN TIME IN EGYPT AND SOUTH AFRICA THEY SHOWED THAT THEIR OLD REPUTATION WAS SAFE IN THE KEEPING OF THE YOUNGER GENERATION.

IN THE PRESENT WAR ASK GENERAL SIR HORACE SMITH-DORRIEN WHAT HE THINKS OF THE BEHAVIOUR OF YOUR REGIMENT ? DISTINCTIONS TOO NUMEROUS TO MENTION, FROM THE VICTORIA CROSS DOWNWARDS, HAVE BEEN WON BY OFFICERS, NON-COMMISSIONED OFFICERS AND MEN.

YOUNG MEN OF CORNWALL, ARE YOU GOING TO LET THESE MEN DEFEND YOUR HOMES AND YOUR DEAR ONES ALONE, WHILE YOU HANG BACK INGLORIOUSLY DOING NOTHING TO HELP ! IT IS YOUR DUTY TO JOIN YOUR COUNTY REGIMENT NOW, AND SO ENSURE THAT FOR A LIFETIME AT LEAST YOUR COUNTRY WILL BE FREE FROM DANGER OF INVASION, AND THAT THOSE WHO HAVE SUFFERED FOR YOU WILL HAVE THEIR LAND CLEARED OF THE BRUTAL HORDES WHO HAVE LAID IT WASTE.

MOTHERS OF CORNWALL, WILL YOU HOLD YOUR SONS BACK ! WILL YOU BY YOUR SELFISH WEAKNESS MARK YOUR SON FOR LIFE WITH THE BRAND OF SHAME, AS ONE WHO WOULD NOT COME FORWARD IN HIS COUNTRY'S NEED.

FATHERS OF CORNWALL, WILL YOU KEEP YOUR SONS WITH YOU BECAUSE THEY HELP YOU IN YOUR BUSINESS, OR ON YOUR FARM ! IF OTHER PARENTS HAD NOT SACRIFICED SOMETHING TO LET THEIR SONS GO FOR YOUR DEFENCE, WHERE WOULD YOUR BUSINESS OR YOUR FARM BE NOW !

COME ALONG THEN LADS !

YOUR COMRADES IN THE

Duke of Cornwall's Light Infantry

HAVE DONE WONDERS.

THEY CALL ON YOU TO MAKE SURE THAT THEIR LABOURS ARE NOT IN VAIN.

GO to the nearest Recruiting Officer, or send a card to the Recruiting Officer at Bodmin, who will give you any information you require.

GOD SAVE THE KING.

West Briton Thursday 1st April 1915

headlined 'Amazing Excuses Made for Not Joining Up', a blacksmith telling Colonel Williams that 'he didn't give a rap if the Germans came there'. 'Colonel Williams declared that he had had his eyes opened more than ever before, and had received some shocks'. At Trewennack, Colonel Williams claimed that there were 63 able bodied men in that area who had not joined up - 'why should these men here (pointing to those in khaki) sacrifice themselves for you 63 lazy fellows... . These men in uniform put their King and country first, and you 63 put your own miserable little wants first and your King and country last'. 'The Welsh miner was putting his King and country before his own miserable local affairs. Why can't you follow that example? It is a crying shame you men in Cornwall should see your brother miners going and laying down their lives, and that you will not go and back them up'. Whether the gallant colonel was striking the right note with the proud Cornish miner is very doubtful. 'Even after these appeals, the recruiter drew a blank, not one recruit being obtained'. The colonel's attitude to farmers who would not volunteer was even more forthright - 'kick them off the land and out of the country'.[8] Wendron parish, according to the colonel, contained 362 eligible men, of which 14 had volunteered - 'it is nothing more or less than a d... disgrace'. The Church then weighed in, with the Reverend Hocking asked 'Were Cornishmen afraid? The two chief occupations Cornishmen were engaged in were mining and fishing, and these required the exhibition of great courage. Why did not the Cornishmen come forward in great numbers? Was it selfishness or cold indifference?... If he was a girl, he would not be seen walking with any man of military age unless he was in khaki. Women could persuade the men to go. If the worst came with all its agony, the blame would lie with the shirkers at home'. Replying, the Reverend Carr disclaimed any cowardice or selfishness on the part of the Cornish. 'He believed that it was due to ignorance of the tremendous thing that they were up against, and of the certainty that if they bowed the knee to the Baal of Germany, all they valued must be swept away with one clean swoop, and of their being nothing but slaves at the mercy of a tyrannical foe'.[9]

If indeed there was an element of indifference among the Cornish in the early stages of the war, a letter to the *Packet* posed the question, what had the older generation done in the years before the war to encourage the young men to prepare for war? The writer answers his own question by asserting that there had been 'nothing but condemnation of everything in the shape of drill or military training for boys at school or of young men in later life... . For the best part of their lives the young men have listened to the thoughtless speeches of their elders about the impossibility of war and the awful waste and extravagance involved in preparation for it'. It seems that a Seth Minards told his elders at a recruiting meeting:
'We've got to go because you've brought this about. We've to wipe up the mess and if the young men must go and wipe it up, an' if for them there's never to be bride-ale nor children, 'tis your doing an' the doin' o' your generation. Why were we brought up one way to be tortured turnin' our conscience to another?'[10]

This surely is further evidence that the war 'came out of the blue' for the average working man. With the benefit of hindsight, it is easy to see why many young Cornishmen not only were taken by surprise by the outbreak of war, but also did not see that it was 'their' war - rather it was something which 'the gentry' had brought about without any reference or explanation to the general public, and the natural first reaction for many would have been that those who had created the crisis could get on with solving it.

Another recruiting rally was held in October, when the band of the Royal Fusiliers accompanied a large party of recruiters, led by the Mayor of Falmouth, A.W. Chard, and Lieut. Col. Hesketh, visited in turn Stithians, Longdowns, Mabe, Constantine, Penryn and Falmouth. The recruiters had a somewhat dispiriting day, despite many eloquent speeches and appeals. Having had no success at Stithians, they also drew a blank at Longdowns, where 'one young man informed a sergeant that he hadn't got any heart, whilst a second gave an excuse that he wanted to wait until the winter was over'. Two names were taken as likely recruits at Mabe, 'but one person who offered his services only possessed one eye - Mr. Chard intends to see if he can be accepted for the Royal Veterinary Corps'. Constantine produced no possible recruits, despite lengthy appeals and even a squabble between the Mayor and Col. Hesketh, the former claiming that they 'had the Germans on the run' and the latter disagreed - 'they had not got them in anything like that condition. They had gained a certain amount of ground and were finding it a very hard task to keep it'. At Penryn the party was met by the Mayor and Corporation, and the local troop of boy scouts, and they all marched to the Town Hall, where a large crowd had assembled. A succession of appeals were made, 'and five men were attested. Five more also promised to enlist, whilst others agreed to seriously consider the matter'. Finishing at Falmouth, a crowd of over 2,000 assembled on the Moor to hear the recruiters. When the Mayor made his appeal, someone in the crowd shouted, 'join up yourself', whereupon the Mayor pointed out that he had been a member of the naval reserve until he reached the age limit, and that at the age of 50, less three months, his way of serving his country was by acting as honorary recruiting officer. He then said, amidst laughter, that the person who had shouted was well known to him in his capacity as chairman of the local bench. Twenty men subsequently gave their names as volunteers.[11]

Falmouth Corporation resolved to make up the wages of any employee who enlisted, if what he received from the army was less than his wages from the Corporation. The example given was of a man earning £1.1s per week working for the Corporation, as opposed to his army pay of 17s 6d.

In October 1915 it was estimated that 20,000 Cornishmen were serving in the Army and Navy, but this figure still left 30,000 of military age who had not volunteered. 'Up and down the county there are thousands of single men of military age who do not offer any reason for not joining the Army, and who stolidly refuse to do so. The call is urgent... If the response is not generous, it will be impossible to avoid conscription'.[12] To try to facilitate recruitment, 'recruiting doctors' were appointed in Falmouth and Penryn. Those wishing to enlist could present themselves at the doctor's residence for medical examination, and if passed fit, could take their papers forthwith to the Recruiting Officer, Major Ellis, at Bank Place, Falmouth.[13] However, if there was a problem in recruiting in Cornwall, Falmouth can be absolved of any responsibility for this, as 74% of the men targeted in the United Borough of Falmouth and Penryn under Lord Derby's recruiting scheme either enlisted, or tried to do so and were rejected - a far higher percentage than in any of the other Cornish parliamentary divisions.[14]

Nationally, it gradually became clear that recruitment could not continue indefinitely on a voluntary basis. As conscription became inevitable, the *Packet* turned its attention to 'the State's claim to the services of married and unmarried men', praising the Government for making it clear that married men 'will not be summoned to the colours while any considerable proportion of eligible single men hang back from volunteering, and prefer to await an opportunity of taking the employment which married men quit when they go to serve King and Country in the army... . There has been a persistent endeavour in the pro-German press in this country to persuade workmen that Lord Derby's recruitment scheme cloaks a 'conspiracy' against trade unionism'.[15] Presumably the reference to the 'pro-German press' is to that part of the press which was broadly supportive of organised labour, and which had been concerned that labour disputes might be brought to an end forcibly by intervention of the military, a fear which the Government dispelled by a specific statement on the subject. To describe this section as 'pro-German', when so many trade unionists had volunteered and indeed died for their country, shows the depth of the bitterness which the strains of war had engendered.

Conscription became inevitable by the end of 1915, and was accompanied by tribunals set up to consider applications for exemptions, and reports of the tribunal's proceedings appeared each week in the *Packet*. The overall impression from these reports is that it was not at all easy to gain exemption from military service, save in cases of extreme hardship, and even then exemption was rarely granted for more than three months. To take at random, for a week, the work of the Falmouth tribunal, a market gardener whose only help had been his brother, who was then at the front, and whose father was bedridden, was told that 'fruit growing is not essential, or can be carried on by female labour'. A grocer who ran a small business to support himself and his crippled mother was told that 'it was a very small business of insufficient importance to permit of the applicant being regarded as indispensable'. A young man in a hardware business said that his father was 75, and could not be expected to run the business in the son's absence. A member of the tribunal told him, 'Don't talk to me about a man of 75 or 80 years of age not being able to render some help in carrying on a small business'. When the applicant pointed out that his father could not lift heavy furniture, he received the somewhat unhelpful advice 'then you must get the people to pack it smaller'. On the other hand, a butcher won total exemption on the grounds that his business was 'a reserved occupation'. When a fruit grower won exemption on the same grounds, the military representative on the panel gave notice of appeal, stating, 'I consider glass a pure luxury. You cannot produce food under glass that you can call cheap food'. One man, calling himself a dock and wharf labourer and a pilot, applied for exemption on the grounds of being in a reserved occupation. The military representative challenged this, claiming that the applicant was in fact a 'quay lumper', and then explained that 'quay lumpers are a group of men who stand at the quay corner and do nothing'. On the application being refused, the man remarked that 'there were young men around the table who ought to be sent up before other people. It was nothing but a b---- fraud'. A young clerk applied for exemption on the grounds that he was the sole support of his widowed mother, who was suffering from consumption. The tribunal asked what would he do concerning his mother if he married, to which the applicant replied that he would continue to support her. 'That would depend on your wife'. 'No, it would not'. 'You are brave now. You wait until you are married'. In this case, exemption was granted. A stonemason made application on the grounds that he was stone deaf in one ear, and had a widowed mother, a widowed sister, and two children to support. The tribunal were not interested in his dependants, but adjourned the case for a medical concerning his alleged loss of hearing. A case dealing with an employee of a laundry, engaged on doing work for military hospitals, resulted in a sharp exchange between the employer and the military representative, who said 'Who is doing the washing in France? Who did it in Gallipoli, where our men were dying of thirst?' The employer: 'If you have wounded soldiers who want work done and there are no men left to do it, they have to suffer. If you have not more sympathy with the wounded in England than that, I can't say much for you'. The military representative: 'How many wounded are there in Falmouth?' The employer: 'I don t know, that is not my business'. A plumber claimed that he was in an exempted occupation, since he worked mainly on ships, but it appeared that the man also worked on his own account in the town, so his application was refused on the grounds that he was not wholly a ship's plumber.[16] One man was exempted on account of his height, or lack of it - 4 feet 8 inches.

The Falmouth Tribunal caused a furore by excluding the press and public from most of their hearings, and would only hear an application in public if the applicant specifically requested it.[18] This caused much adverse press comment, and it is not clear why the Falmouth Tribunal, alone of the local tribunals, took this course.

At a meeting of the Cornwall War Agricultural Committee in May 1916, the difficulties suffered by agriculture as a result of the conscription of so many workers were discussed. A protest was made by Mr. W. Lanyon that it was necessary to recruit Irish labourers to take the place of those called to the colours, 'at a higher wage than our own men had been receiving. The Irish should be kept in their own country, especially after recent experiences. He would rather let his produce go than employ one of them'. General dissatisfaction was expressed with the work of the tribunals, and it was claimed that large swathes of land were derelict because there was no labour to work it. Particular anger was expressed at what was perceived to be the bias of the tribunals against farmers' sons, and it was claimed that 'not sufficient emphasis had been given to the question of whether he (the farmer's son) was indispensable on the farm'.[19]

The coming of conscription did not put an end to the complaints that too many young men were still not in the Army or the Navy. The *Daily Mail* attacked the work of the Falmouth and East Kerrier tribunals, the clear inference being that whilst the tribunals were severe on working class applicants for exemption, they were much more tolerant as regards those from a middle class background. The *Mail* claimed that 'there is plenty of scope for a strong comb in and around Falmouth. The Falmouth tribunals have been the cause of a great deal of discontent, and the action of the town court in shielding men who ought to go to the Army but who have kept out of it through local interest, has been the talk of the countryside for months. On high days and holidays an extraordinary number of young men may be seen lounging about the town, smartly dressed and killing time in all manner of pleasant ways... Many of the young men who are thus evading war service are the envied and cherished young gentlemen who months ago dropped quietly into the Royal Naval Volunteer Reserve with the promise of an 'easy job' which has not yet taken form. With a most commendable patience they are waiting for the country to call upon their valuable services. They are not even in uniform - but they are in the RNVR and the local recruiting officer, who has been fishing industriously for them for some time, has not been able to hook more than one or two of them out of their strictly preserved water... This naval work, of course, is very important, particularly at a port of the importance and the intricacy of Falmouth - if the men belonging to the service are in any way skilled at their work. But a number of these young stowaways know nothing whatever about the work they have been able to find for themselves (with the aid of a little local influential 'push')... 'If any one of them went out in a boat and a bit of a sea happened to be on', said one of the officers to me, 'he'd be helpless with sea sickness".[20] The *Briton* commented, 'Often it has been said that half the people in Cornwall do not realise the gravity of the crisis through which the Empire is passing', and then went on to claim that many young men were applying to the tribunals for exemption 'for trifling and absurd reasons', and that many would not be regarded as 'indispensable' if only greater advantage was taken of the available pool of female labour.[21]

In July 1915, a National Register had been compiled of all men and women, not already in the forces, of working age, with the intention of matching jobs with labour. Six months later the *Briton* was complaining that little use had been made of the register - 'going on at this rate, we shall not have organised the nation for war purposes until long after the war is over'.[22] Strikes in important sectors of industry were treated with disgust in the Cornish press, claiming that the general public 'are not in the mood to risk defeat or delay victory for a section of the men who have remained at home in comfortable berths at high wages'.[23] Another cause of discontent were the vagaries of the various tribunals' decisions. The *Briton* was incensed that a huntsman of a local hunt was fourteen days late in applying for exemption, a fact which was overlooked by the tribunal, and was granted exemption. 'There was no long questioning as to whether the acting hunt manager could find a man ineligible for the Army, and, of course, no one even thought of suggesting that the war was more important than fox hunting'. The *Briton* went on to compare this case with the close scrutiny given by tribunals to applications by farmers, tradesmen and others when failure to obtain exemption may result in financial ruin. 'County clerks, schoolmasters, experts from many businesses, and the small tradesman must go. To a huntsman there is granted 'exemption in accordance with the military recommendation'. Perhaps this is an official interpretation of the glib phrase 'equality of sacrifice".[24]

Another hurdle erected by local tribunals which applicants had to surmount was, 'is this business necessary in the national interest?' The answer in the vast majority of small businesses was bound to be 'No', but in fact, as the *Briton* pointed out, there was no provision in the regulations for this test to be applied. The basic conditions on which the applicant had to satisfy the tribunal in order to succeed in his application for exemption were threefold:

1   That the applicant was the sole proprietor of the business.
2   That his family, exclusively or mainly, depended on it, and
3   That it was impossible to find a substitute

It followed from these conditions that the owner of a one man business should succeed in his appeal if, by drafting him into the Army, serious hardship would be caused to his dependants. This was very different from 'the national interest' test.[25]   However, the Cornwall Appeal Tribunal, to which appeals went from the decisions of local tribunals, refused to back down, even when asked for an explanation by the Local Government Board, maintaining that 'only in the most exceptional circumstances can it be held to be in the national interest at the present time that single men physically fit between the ages of 18½ and 25 should be retained in civil employment'.[26]   The *Briton* also raised the question, whether Cornwall was providing a larger number of men for the Army and Navy than most other counties in proportion to population. The paper claimed that the local tribunals were sending men to the forces who could ill be spared at home, whilst in other counties men in the same situation were being exempted. Was it possible that the tribunals were being more strict in Cornwall than elsewhere because of the allegation that early in the war Cornishmen did not answer the call as readily as some other parts of the country? If this was so, it was an injustice because in only a few areas had Cornishmen been slow to volunteer, and that was mainly due to so many men of military age working abroad as miners.[27]   The editor again took the local tribunals to task, claiming that they were acting under the direction of the Army, 'whose requests they must carry out without regard to the terms of the Military Service Acts... The applicant and the military representative stand on the same level in relation to the Tribunal. They are like the plaintiff and defendant in a civil action. But too many tribunals have regarded the applicant as in the wrong and the military representative as in a kind of partnership with the Tribunals in serving the State'. Until a High Court case decided that it was unlawful, it had been the practice for tribunals to require the applicant to leave the room whilst they considered the case, whilst allowing the military representative to remain and, presumably, join in the discussion. The decision of the High Court 'constitutes another reminder that the Tribunal is a Court of Justice and not a branch of the recruiting office'.[28]

Each man had to undergo a medical examination for military service, after which he was issued with a classification certificate. The categories were:

A   Fit for general service
B   Fit for service abroad, but not fit for general service
C   Fit for service at home only
R   Rejected, and therefore exempted from military service.[29]

By the end of 1917, the armed forces were desperate for men, and those between the ages of 40 and 50 were compulsorily graded, whether or not they were in 'exempted occupations'. The Minister for National Service, Sir Auckland Geddes, said, 'The war might drift on into 1920 and after, if we do not pull ourselves together for the mightiest effort of our history. We have seen behind our little extravagances the waste of human energy... New hats alone absorb the work of millions of fingers and whatever effect they may have, that effect certainly does not include helping the Army to beat the enemy'.

Being a conscientious objector was no easy option. One such got short shrift from the Falmouth Tribunal, who 'considered that it was a disgrace to breed such people'.[30]   The depth of the antagonism towards conscientious objectors was illustrated by the passing by Penryn Corporation of a resolution reading: 'That this Council wishes to place on record its strong objection to the preferential treatment to conscientious objectors now at Princetown, who have refused to take their share of national responsibility in the Great War, and object to the privileges they are enjoying, and which are not granted to our brave fighting boys in the trenches'. Councillor Andrew said that 'the Government had passed a law that fit men of military age should join HM Forces and men were fighting as never Britishers fought before; yet the Government had removed from Princetown one set of criminals and put a worse set in their place. Why should these vermin have such liberties? - (laughter). They were not only shirkers, but liars - (renewed laughter)'. Councillor W.J. Crothers could not understand why the clergy of all denominations were exempt from call up. 'Why should his boy and their boys be exposed to all dangers and death, simply because he did not wear the clerical cloth? - (hear, hear)... Those who were not willing to take their part in battle he would place under worse conditions than our men in France were placed in, for they should dig trenches, and be up to their necks in mud, much less their knees, and then they might change their opinion and be willing to take the side of the brave soldiers - (hear, hear)'. There was much more in the same vein, no one speaking against the resolution.[31]

Bernard Walke, in his delightful book *Twenty Years at St. Hilary,* described vividly what it was like to be on the receiving end of such hatred. He was addressing a peace meeting in Penzance, when it was broken up by about one hundred and fifty naval personnel under the command of an officer, and the room and furniture completely smashed. Walke wrote, 'I had met angry crowds before, but never had I faced hate as I did that night, a black and sullen hate that was beyond reason or appeal'. He and his wife escaped serious injury only due to the protection of two soldiers on leave from France, who were quite prepared to take on all the sailors at once.[32] Walke visited the conscientious objectors in the prison at Princetown, and has left a vivid account:

'I addressed a meeting of the colony of six hundred men. Was there ever gathered together so strange a collection of individuals? Quiet Quakers who sat unmoved while men stood up and shouted round them, wild looking men from the Clyde and Rhondda Valley whose hopes for the regeneration of society lay in a class war, strange melancholy men whose message was the immediate coming of the Messiah and the end of the world, men of all trades and professions, mathematicians, scholars, musicians, actors, miners and farm labourers, with nothing to unite them but a refusal to bear arms in the present war. I was distressed and dismayed by the clash and conflict of theories and personalities with which I was confronted. Some brandished Bibles, accusing me of not knowing the Word of God revealed in the Book of Daniel, others with red flags proclaimed me as a traitor for not accepting class war and the dictatorship of the proletariat. I had come, expecting to find, in this assembly of youth, some hope for the future, but failed to discover among these men who talked ceaselessly, waving flags and Bibles, the kind of material out of which a new world might be constructed'.[33]

One unusual calling to the colours occurred when a hundred Cornishmen were recruited to assist in the loading of coal at London docks, at the behest of the Admiralty. There had been considerable delay in the loading, to the detriment of the fleet, and the leaders of the Coal Porters' Union raised no objection to outside labour being brought in, provided that they joined the Union, which the Cornish recruits did. However, on the Cornish arriving at the docks, 'they were met by a large number of coal heavers, and their friends, who exhibited a hostile attitude towards the newcomers'. Ugly scenes developed, and the Cornishmen were withdrawn, but not before the Union had agreed that the existing workforce would meet the full requirements of the Admiralty. 'The authorities agreed to pay the Cornishmen's fares home, with pay at the rate of 30s a week and 30s bonus'.[34]

NOTES

[1] WB, 25.1.1915, p2
[2] WB, 8.2.1915, p2
[3] FP, 6.11.1914, p6

[4] WB, 22.3.1915, p2
[5] WB, 1.2.1915, p2
[6] WB, 3.5.1915, p2

[7] FP, 2.4.1915, p2
[8] FP, 26.3.1915, p6
[9] FP, 21.5.1915, p5
[10] FP, 6.8.1915, p4
[11] FP, 8.10.1915, p6
[12] WB, 4.10.1915, p2
[13] FP, 3.12.1915, p3
[14] WB, 30.12.1915, p7
[15] FP, 26.11.1915, p3
[16] FP, 17.3.1916, p3
[17] FP, 19.1.1917, p4
[18] WB, 13.3.1916, p2
[19] FP, 26.5.1916
[20] Daily Mail, 16.11.1916, reprinted in FP, 17.11.1916 p3
[21] WB, 10.1.1916, p2

[22] WB, 17.1.1916, p2
[23] WB, 17.1.1916, p2
[24] WB, 12.6.1916, p2
[25] WB, 11.9.1916, p2
[26] WB, 23.9.1916, p2
[27] WB, 1.11.1917, p2
[28] WB, 12.2.1917, p2
[29] Certificate held by the Royal Cornwall Polytechnic Society, Falmouth
[30] FP, 9.2.1917, p3
[31] FP, 4.5.1917, p3
[32] Bernard Walke, *Twenty Years At St. Hilary*, Truran, 2002, p98
[33] Bernard Walke, ibid., pp103-104
[34] FP, 6.8.1915, p5

CHAPTER VII

WOMEN'S WAR WORK

Public meetings were held in Falmouth to encourage women to undertake some sort of war service. At these meetings, in which Mrs. Hext of Trebah was very prominent, great emphasis was placed on there being nothing 'demeaning' in physical labour - 'there was nothing to be ashamed of in having to work in overalls or to put on old clothes', and women were encouraged particularly to take the place of farm labourers who had volunteered, for which they would receive fair pay, although 'they could not expect to get the same pay as men'. At a meeting at Budock, after Mrs. Hext had listed all the farming tasks which women could undertake, a lady tartly interjected 'I do not believe that the farmers want women - (laughter)'.[1] The importance of women to the war economy was stressed at a meeting at Mawnan, where Mr. Justice Rowlatt raised the question of what would happen after the war, and painted a rather stark, if as it turned out truthful, picture:

'It was agreed by those most competent to judge that after the war there would be a period of severe distress and depression. That was absolutely certain. At present enormous sums of money were being borrowed and flung about the country. That must come to a stop and the money must be repaid. It would be no use going about and begging people to give them employment, because they would not be able to do so. It would be a question of whom they could dispense with. Therefore, it was most important that every shilling should be saved now'.[2]

A Miss Deane, of the Board of Trade, addressed a meeting at the Town Hall on the subject of 'War Work for Women'. She warned that middle class women would have to get used to running their homes without the aid of domestic servants, a very large number of whom had registered to do war service work, 'and no doubt hundreds more would be called upon to undertake such work, as they were able to stand the longer hours of factory labour better than many people'. She went on to urge her audience to take up shop work, claiming that in the big towns the large stores were almost entirely run by women, although there was a snag - 'it is extraordinary to find how few women could keep accounts properly, knew anything about book keeping or could write a good commercial letter. Very few people could really type well and knew little or nothing about shorthand'. Miss Deane then went on to call for volunteers as cooks, teachers, dispensers of medicines, farm and horticultural workers, and motor drivers, although 'it was no use learning motor driving unless they also learnt to do running repairs'. She also suggested that 'they might study the proper way to cook vegetables, and to make use of those foods that could take the place of meat'. As a final point, she warned against the better off 'offering to do work for a mere nominal sum, for it would have a serious effect on their fellow women who had got to earn their own living'.[3]

At a meeting of the Cornwall War Agricultural Committee in May 1916, it was reported that in Cornwall a total of 4,044 women were employed in some sort of war work, of which about 2,500 were engaged on the land.[4] There is no doubt that one of the great difficulties in securing the employment of women on the land, was the prejudice of farmers against such employment, despite the fact that most had wives - 'very few women worked harder than the farmer's wife did at the present time' - and for a long time there were many more applications for agricultural work by women than there were posts to fill. Such work also required a change of attitude by some ladies - Mr. Carkeek 'attended a (women's recruiting) meeting where a lady came in twenty minutes late and left twenty minutes after, because she had five o'clock tea'. A farmer, Mr. Liddicoat, stated that it should be 'just as popular in the near future for young women to milk cows as to play the piano, and they would have more respect for the one who could do it'.[5]

A leader in the *Briton* defended the farmers, who 'have been placed in a false position in the public estimation through the whole of the circumstances not being understood'. It was pointed out that women who were volunteering for farm work were qualified to milk the cows, make the butter and cream and attend to the poultry, but these tasks were already being performed by the wives and daughters of farmers. What the volunteers could not do is to replace the men who had joined the forces in working a team of horses, looking after the cattle and 'the other hard work that falls to the lot of farm hands'.[6] The resistance of farmers continued, and at a further meeting of the War Agricultural Committee, Mrs. Hext complained that farmers would not say with what kind of work women could help, and indeed had expressed no desire to employ women at all, so it was no surprise that women at that time were not coming forward enthusiastically for agricultural work.[7] A 'sinister reason' for the farmers' reluctance was suggested by the *Briton* - if women proved useful on farms, this would weaken the argument for keeping the sons of farmers at home.[8]

By 1918, women working in agriculture had been organised into the Women's Land Army, and the numbers had grown to such an extent that there were 40 or 50 'gangs' working all over the county, some of whom were engaged on thatching and sheep shearing in addition to normal agricultural work. The Executive Committee reported that 'recruits from Wales had proved thoroughly unsatisfactory and had been returned... There had been a few naughty undisciplined girls, but so far only three had been dismissed'. There were 414 members of the WLA in Cornwall, of which 290 were engaged in agriculture, 76 in forage and 48 in timber. 'The greatest of the difficulties they had to face was the prejudice of Cornish farmers against women labour. This had been broken down in many instances by the efficient work and good behaviour of some of the girls, but in some districts it strongly existed'. There was a suggestion that Cornish farmers did not like the WLA because if women were available to do men's work, more of the men would have to join the forces, and it was claimed that young men asked women not to join the WLA as it would mean that the men would have to go into the Army.[9] Certainly if any of the women had illusions about the romance of the countryside, they soon lost them; what they found was hard manual labour, dirty and sometimes dangerous conditions, long hours, primitive accommodation, low pay and strict regimentation, quite apart from male prejudice. The WLA was finally disbanded on the 30th November 1919.[10]

Whilst the majority of Cornish women engaged in war work were employed in agriculture, they were to be found in many other vital sectors. Whilst there were no local munitions factories, Falmouth women were found in every occupation, including ambulance drivers, shop assistants, postal clerks, milk roundswomen, as well as in the newly formed women's sections of the armed forces and the police. Many of the nursing staff in the naval and military hospitals in the town were young women who were not nurses by profession, but had volunteered, and after basic training, assisted the fully trained staff. These volunteers were known as V.A.D.s, and were vital to the running of hospitals, both in this country and where the armies were fighting abroad. One of them, Vera Brittain, was bitterly critical of the rules and regulations of the nursing profession:

'Its regulations and its values are still so Victorian that we even have to do our work in fancy dress, struggling perpetually with an exasperating seven piece uniform, always changing caps, collars, aprons, cuffs and waist belts that accumulate germs and get lost in the laundry, or collecting the innumerable studs, clips and safety pins required to hold the cumbrous outfit together, instead of wearing one loose-necked, short sleeved overall that could be renewed every day'.[11]

WWI ambulances in Falmouth Docks - note women drivers

It was to be another fifty years or more before the profession could be persuaded to adopt such suitable dress.

During the war, more than 1.5 million women eventually replaced men in the workplace, freeing the latter for the armed forces.[12] This huge contribution by women to the war effort was far more instrumental than all the efforts of the suffragettes in bringing about a sea change in the national consciousness, which allowed the granting of votes to women in the 1918 election to go through as a recognised right. It brought to an abrupt end the furious pre-war debate on female suffrage, and fundamentally improved the status of women, despite some remaining die-hard attitudes. The Chamber of Commerce provided an example of such die-hard attitudes. After the war was ended, the Chamber was considering attracting a factory to Falmouth to employ female labour, but at least one voice opposed the idea on the basis that a factory would diminish the pool of domestic servants available to the middle class.[13] The battle for sex equality had only just begun, but after women had spread their wings in the Great War, things would never be the same again.

NOTES

[1] FP, 6.8.1915, p2
[2] FP, 6.8.1915, p2
[3] FP, 24.9.1915, p6
[4] FP, 26.5.1916
[5] WB, 29.7.1915, p6
[6] WB, 8.11.1915, p2
[7] WB, 13.1.1916, p4

[8] WB, 1.5.1916, p2
[9] FP, 28.6.1918
[10] WB, 9.10.1919, p2
[11] Vera Brittain, *Testament of Youth*, p453
[12] Richard van Emden & Steve Humphries, *All Quiet On The Home Front*, p118-119
[13] FP, 22.8.1919, p4

CHAPTER VIII

IN FOR THE LONG HAUL - 1916

The New Year dawned more in a state of grim determination than in hope. In January, Lord Lonsdale made a speech in which he forecast that the war would be over by August. The *Briton* begged to differ - 'Had the nation a year ago thought less of when the war would end and prepared more munitions and men, we should have been further forward than we are now'.[1] However, by April 1916, some were already looking, somewhat gloomily, towards the commercial and industrial situation in Cornwall after the war. Someone, signing himself as 'Cornubian', asked, what was being done by industry to replace with home produced goods, those items, totalling £80 million pounds worth in 1913, formerly imported from Germany? Fearing a recession in the mining industry, the writer saw no future in relying on tourism - 'Instead of setting out parks and promenades, money might now more usefully be devoted to the deepening of rivers and the extension of docks. As an example, Falmouth can be under no delusions that the Dutch liners will continue to make the town a port of call after the war, for no inducement by way of provision of better landing facilities etc. are offered to the shipping companies to do so. A few weeks ago at a meeting of the Falmouth Chamber of Commerce, it was suggested in a rather vague manner that factories should be laid down to provide work for the large number of Falmouth men who will return from the war. But few people can be optimistic enough to believe that such suggestions will get beyond the consideration stage'.[2]

The German air raids on London and east coast resorts had a considerable psychological effect, and even as far west from the area of these raids as Falmouth, precautions were taken in the event of a raid. A siren was fixed in the electric light works, which would be sounded together with the hooter in the foundry in the event of a raid, and it was announced that gas pressure would be reduced to a quarter of its usual strength and electric light would be switched off.[3]

The war could not interrupt either high or low culture. The well known Falmouth artist, C. Napier Hemy, exhibited a picture at the Royal Academy, which was very favourably reviewed in the *Packet*. Entitled 'AD 1915', the paper described it:

'The scene represents an incident which happened somewhere in the North Sea. Morning is breaking, and the sullen looking clouds are clearing off, whilst there is a lively sea. A German submarine has been caught on the surface by a British torpedo boat and the inevitable duel follows, both craft having hoisted their colours. The engagement takes place at close quarters and the wash of the sea between the lead coloured German and her black grimy looking opponent develops into a tumble which is treated with the masterly skill that has helped to make Mr. Hemy so famous. It is a Hemy sea, and what better tribute can be paid to the artist? There is something fascinating about the little torpedo boat, and it helps to increase that spirit of thankfulness for, and the calm trust in, our Navy, which is being felt at present by Britishers'. In pre-war days Hemy had watched torpedo boats exercising in Falmouth Bay and at that time had made the sketches which enabled him to produce the painting.[4]

At the other end of the cultural scale, the Princess Pavilion proudly announced that 'quite a unique entertainment is being presented here this week. Elroy, the armless wonder, is a veritable marvel,

Torpedo Flotilla in Falmouth Harbour, July 1910

and the wonderful way in which he draws cartoons, paints pictures, gives an exhibition of trick shooting, and performs a cornet solo - all with the feet - must be seen to be believed... Nothing better, pictorially or dramatically, has been seen in Falmouth than the fine film depicting 'The Shooting of Dan McGrew...' Tonight and tomorrow 'The Heart of a Painted Woman' will be screened and should meet with considerable success'.[5]

With the vast influx of soldiers, Royal Naval and Merchant Navy personnel, prostitution, never unknown in a port, was a cause for concern. A public meeting in Falmouth resolved to employ a 'trained worker in connection with preventative and rescue work' among actual or potential 'fallen women and girls' at a cost of £100 per year.[6] Another public meeting of the Falmouth Social Welfare Association, formerly the Female Rescue Society, was addressed by a Miss Hudson, who said, 'it would be misleading for her to even infer that they had in Falmouth none of the colossal evils found in other places. If they took the hand-to-mouth people of Falmouth with a number of the hand-to-mouth population of the east of London, they would find as much depravity, immorality, degradation and squalor in their town as would be found in the city'. Somewhat bizarrely, Miss Hudson said that there was a feeling that this was due 'to climatic reasons, and she had heard a very great deal of the cause put down to the Gulf Stream'. She seemed on somewhat stronger ground when she said that it might be due to the fact that Falmouth was a port and a railway terminus, together with poor and insanitary housing. 'With regard to the streets of Falmouth, all she had seen were a few giddy loud girls making themselves cheap, but watch as carefully as she could, she did not see the professional element about'. But Miss Hudson went on to say that, Falmouth being a port at which all nationalities mingled, 'certain conduct was carried on under the surface, hidden under the cloak of so-called respectability, by married and single women and girls. It cropped up in most unlooked for quarters, and was carried on under the guise of friendship, friendly calls, and some people condoned it and connived at it'. Apparently, what were needed were 'clean souled, public spirited men and women of the town insisting on one moral standard', and a centre house where the fallen women could be looked after, medically and morally. In defence of the town, the Mayor pointed out that they had made a start on the housing problem just before the war in building 44 workmen's dwellings, but that the work had been stopped by the war, and would be resumed as a matter of urgency once hostilities ceased.[7]

Tragedy struck on 16th April, when one of Falmouth's leading doctors, Dr. G.E. Lanyon, committed suicide by taking prussic acid, leaving a wife and five children, the youngest only six weeks old. He had an extensive practice in the town and numerous appointments, including medical officer to the Port Sanitary Authority and at Falmouth Hospital.[8] Another well known resident to die, in May, was Lady Fayrer, the widow of Surgeon-General Sir Joseph Fayrer, one of the last survivors of the siege of Lucknow in the Indian Mutiny of 1857. She and her late husband had retired to Falmouth many years previously, and her husband had done so much to promote the town as a health resort that he had been admitted to the Freedom of the Borough. Lady Fayrer had written briefly about her experiences in the famous siege:

'I recall a day during the siege when I was lying ill in bed, in a small room opening on to a verandah, and my friend, Mrs. George Boileau, was sitting on the bed talking to me. As we were talking a shell fell close to my bed just inside the verandah. Supposing it to be only a round shot, Mrs Boileau and I went on talking when suddenly the shell, a 9 lb. shrapnel full of bullets, burst, and Mrs. Boileau ran to fetch my husband. Mrs Boileau and I had been too close to the shell, and when it burst the fragments and bullets must have gone over our heads, as they were found at the other side of the room'. Lady Fayrer also recounted how her one year old son had been shot in the leg during the siege, and that she had kept the bullet. A redoubtable daughter of Britannia indeed.[9]

Week after week the *Packet* recorded the deaths in action of local men. A Falmouth man went down with Lord Kitchener on HMS *Hampshire,* when the cruiser was sunk carrying the Minister for War to Russia.[10] Immediately following this, seven Falmouth men were lost at Jutland, the biggest naval battle the world has ever seen. Four of these men lost their lives when the battlecruiser *Indefatigable* blew up with the loss of over a thousand lives.[11] Many men killed at the front or at sea had made what were known as 'soldiers' wills', which dispensed with most of the usual legal requirements for a valid will. These wills are often rather moving documents as, stripped of the usual dry legal language, they convey exactly what was important to the testator. One of these was the will of Lieut. The Hon. Piers Stewart St. Aubyn, brother of Lord St. Levan, who was killed in Flanders. Written in his own hand in the trenches, the Hon. St. Aubyn gave bequests to his servants, with a request that his family should 'look after them if necessary'. He then left to his brother 'all racing and coursing cups and plates, to be made heirlooms. Hoping my collection of china cats will remain intact. I wish no one to wear mourning for me for more than one month, and I desire that no abstention shall be made from shooting, dancing, parties and amusements generally for more than one month. I ask my sisters, Audrey Ponsonby and Evelyn Alcock, to see that my dog, Captain, is kept in comfort all his life - always, if possible, with Mrs. Painter'.[12]

The Easter Rising in Dublin seems to have been of little interest in Cornwall. The *Briton* devoted a small paragraph on page 5 to it, merely stating that order had been restored and the ringleaders shot.[13]

The captain of HMS *Falmouth* proposed to the Corporation that the colours flown by the ship at the recent battle of Jutland should be held in Falmouth, and the offer was gratefully accepted.[14] A casket to hold the colours was made on board the ship, but before this could be handed over, the *Falmouth* was sunk by a submarine in the North Sea, with the loss of eleven of the crew, and the casket containing the colours went down with the ship. The *Falmouth* was a light cruiser with a

2nd November 1911. Captian Grant and Offers of H.M.S. Falmouth entertain the Mayor (F. J. Bowles) and Members of the Town Council on board.

H.M.S. Falmouth

crew of 390, being laid down in 1910 and joining the fleet in 1911. Her first, slightly dubious, claim to fame arose very early in the war. Because of the danger of mines and submarines, the Grand Fleet had taken up station at Scapa Flow in the Orkneys when war was declared, from where it could blockade the German fleet in its North Sea ports. However, Scapa Flow itself had no defences against submarine attack in September 1914, and everyone, from Admiral Jellicoe downwards, was aware of the damage which a U-boat could do if it managed to get into the Flow. On the 1st September as dusk was falling, those on the *Falmouth* thought that they saw the periscope of a submarine in the anchorage, and at once opened fire. Immediately many ships began to 'spot' U-boats and shells were fired in all directions, some landing and exploding on farms and fields on adjoining islands. Admiral Jellicoe decide that the safest option was to take his vast armada to sea, even though darkness was falling rapidly, and with black funnel smoke adding to the thickening murk, the dreadnoughts had to feel their way out to the Pentland Firth. In the meantime the *Falmouth* and other light cruisers and destroyers were racing up and down, signalling new 'sightings' and generally adding to the existing chaos and mayhem. By considerable seamanship, with no navigational lights and visibility dropping at times to less than a hundred yards, the entire fleet got to sea without mishap. As it transpired, neither then nor at any time during the war did a U-boat penetrate Scapa Flow.[15] Later the *Falmouth* played an active part at Jutland, possibly scoring a hit with a torpedo on a German battlecruiser,[16] but a few weeks later she was hit by four torpedoes, which it seems was the number usually required to make certain of sinking a modern warship, which could usually make port for repairs when hit by one or two.[17]

The passing of the Daylight Saving Act was welcomed. It was appreciated that it would diminish the use of electric and gas lighting by one hour each day, thereby making an enormous saving in coal. 'The inconveniences that are bound to arise through the altering of clocks, watches and our own habits are well worth undergoing in order to achieve that'.[18] Immediately on it coming into effect, its benefits were acknowledged - 'The constant wonder is that we did not resort to it years ago. Under the new arrangement there are long, light evenings which are very pleasant during the delightful weather we are experiencing... No one suffers by the alteration - except the gas companies, and even they welcome it owing to the trouble there is in getting coal... It is pretty certain that 'summer time' has come to stay'. It seems that the idea had been objected to by farmers, one reason being that they feared that cows would refuse to be milked an hour earlier.[19] The restrictions under the Lighting Order were extended to include the chiming of public clocks - 'their notes would be audible at a far greater distance in the air above the towns... It would be the height of folly to darken the towns and let the public clocks chime and strike'. It seems that Zeppelins could remain stationary in the air with their engines stopped.[20] Certain places were exempted from the lighting restrictions, such as Falmouth gas works, Pendennis Castle, the Hornworks, and Trevethan Camp, which it may be thought would have made a nonsense of attempts to hide the town from Zeppelins, had any managed to find their way to Cornwall.[21] One highly indignant old lady was fined 7s 6d although she claimed that what the constable saw was not a chink in her blinds but the reflection of the moon on her window.[22] It appears that Zeppelins were the 'bogeymen' of the Great War, their psychological effect extending far further than their range. The Penryn Corporation were concerned about the danger of air raids, arising from a recent 'false alarm' when there had been a rumour of a Zeppelin in the area. Mr Geach thought that it would be wise to insure the town clock. 'It was the only building of a respectable nature that the Council possessed and he would be sorry to see it knocked over'.[23]

The local justices may have been incensed, if they subscribed to *Truth* magazine, to read a paragraph under the heading 'Reprehensible Tenderness':

'The Falmouth magistrates have been severely criticised for their reprehensible tenderness to a tradesman who had been convicted on clear evidence of harbouring a sailor. The evidence was of such a nature that a severe punishment was obviously required. However, the offender was let off with a fine of £7 10s, a decision which was scandalous, as the mischievous business of which he was convicted is known to be exceedingly lucrative. The strange leniency of the magistrates was the more to be censured as the naval authorities had earnestly begged them to take 'a most severe' view of the case. Commander Tower publicly protested in court, pointing out that the penalty was a 'flea-bite'.'[24]

A rather strange case to come before the bench was that of a governess, Helen Wright, staying in Falmouth on her way to take up a post in St. Mawes, who was brought before the court for refusing to complete the form required under war regulations of everyone staying in a hotel or guesthouse. The only information required by the form was her full name, her nationality (which was British) and her signature. Miss Wright flatly refused to complete the form, despite the efforts of persuasion both of the guesthouse proprietor, a police constable, and later at the police station of the inspector. She would give no reason for her refusal, which she maintained when brought before the bench, and was sentenced to a fine of £1 or, in default, ten days imprisonment. History does not relate whether she then relented.[25] When a one legged man was convicted by the bench of wearing naval decorations to which he was not entitled, it was then revealed that he had been convicted for fraud, under twelve different names, and had served sixteen terms of imprisonment. This then became seventeen, with a sentence of six months.[26] In the early twentieth century, a bench of magistrates had very considerable autonomy, and to a large extent administered the law as they saw fit. On the same day the Falmouth bench adopted somewhat different attitudes to two cases before them. A group of boys, aged 8 to 11, convicted of breaking and entering, were dealt with sternly, each being sentenced to six strokes of the birch. A young woman, accused of 'indecent behaviour', was fined 10s, but in her case the bench tempered justice with mercy, telling her that the sum would be remitted if she went back to her parents. 'They were sorry to see a young girl in such a position, and if she did not be careful, it would mean the start on the road to ruin'.[27] In another case involving juveniles, the magistrates extended their powers to hand down a sentence for which there could have been no basis in law. Twins, brother and sister aged 8, were convicted of picking pockets; sentences of corporal punishment for boys were quite usual then and the boy received four strokes of the birch. Corporal punishment for females had been abolished for a hundred years, but that did not prevent the bench ordering the small girl to be whipped by her mother'.[28] The overall drop in crime since the war began continued, and for the first time for thirteen years, there were no prisoners for trial at the Quarter Sessions in October. As a result, the chairman was presented with a pair of white kid gloves 'in token of the county's immunity from crime'.[29]

Surprise was expressed that each of the children in the workhouse, under the control of the Falmouth Board of Guardians, cost the ratepayers 11s 9d per week for maintenance, of which 2s was spent on clothes. 'In no working man's family could the same rate of expenditure be kept up. A man and his wife and four children, if they were provided for on the same scale, would need an income of £3 10s a week... .The average wage in the county for working men is not more than 24s a week... . It is passing strange that so much care is lavished on children when they are paupers and so little is thought of them when they are not'.[30] The *Briton* had it in for the Board of Guardians again over the provision of butter to the inmates of the workhouse rather than margarine. Having pointed out that margarine had taken the place of butter on the tables of most families, the *Briton* went on, 'There are inmates of workhouses who might be expected to follow the same course. Some of them were not so delicately nurtured, either, as to justify any objection on their part... . Healthy paupers ought to share in the deprivations which the war demands. Many poor people outside the workhouses are feeling the times very hard, for all have not money coming from the Army, the Navy, or munition works'.[31]

Over one hundred delegates attended in Falmouth the annual meeting of the Cornwall West District of the United Methodist Church, and the presiding officer, Mr. W.J. Nicholls, delivered a sombre assessment of the state of Methodism. The Church had been forced to accept compulsory military service, 'a thing they loathed in their peace days', dislocation of trade, curtailment of expenditure, the darkening of streets, 'and the State had commandeered the railways, ships and factories for its services. These things were all a part of the price they were paying, and the sum total had not yet been reached. It would come later in the presence of the maimed and wounded, in stricken households, in desolated homes, and in the life and death struggle of thousands for the very existence of life itself.' In the face of this apocalyptic vision, Mr. Nicholls wondered what part the Church could play, bearing in mind that even before the war membership was decreasing, Sunday Schools diminishing, and this trend was accelerating. 'The Nonconformist conscience had ceased to be a terror to their legislators, and gradual indifference to their preaching and teaching was everywhere apparent'. He went on to claim that they had been living 'a life of ease and rejoicing in their worldly possessions, turning their religion into a matter of ceremonial observances, and spending their energies upon trivialities'. He ended this depressing picture with the somewhat Delphic pronouncement that 'it was only through death that they could reach their true life, and that it was only through failure that they could reach their truest success'.[32]

'Spy mania'continued to flourish. Anyone of German extraction was, in the public's mind, a potential spy, and there was 'a very large attendance' at a public meeting on the Moor to consider 'the enemy alien question'. The motion put before the meeting was for the internment and/or deportation 'of all persons of German or other enemy extraction, whether naturalised or not', and went on to say that such people should not be allowed to live or trade anywhere within the Empire after the war. The Mayor claimed that the brother of the German general who brought the case against Nurse Edith Cavell 'was now walking the streets of London smoking a fat cigar... . There were something like 23,000 Germans loose in the kingdom and of these 10,000 were roaming about London'. The loss of the battleships *Formidable* and *Bulwark*, that of the liner *Lusitania*, and the death of Lord Kitchener were all put down to the nefarious activities of spies. 'The motion was unanimously carried, the Mayor remarking that if anyone had the temerity to vote against it he would never had got home'.[33] Spy fever spilled over from Falmouth into Mylor, where the parish council debated and passed a resolution that all enemy aliens 'whether naturalised or not' should be interned. It was pointed out that a harmless Austrian gentleman had for a long time been a resident in Mylor, but all the members, bar one, thought that no exceptions should be made. It was alleged that there were 'men of German extraction in Government offices' and that these should be rooted out as a matter of urgency. The most prominent victim of this campaign against those of German extraction had been Prince Louis of Battenberg, who was First Sea Lord at the outbreak of the war. The Mylor Council pronounced as a fact that 'the country was honeycombed with spies', before going on to discuss the state of repair of the village pump[34]. Anxious not to be left out, the Falmouth Corporation passed a resolution urging the Government to cancel the naturalisation of all those British citizens who originally came from what were now enemy countries and to intern them. One member claimed that Kitchener's death had been greeted 'with great ecstasy in a certain place in Falmouth where two or three employees of doubtful nationality clapped their hands in glee'.[35] In none of these cases was the question of definition of 'German extraction' raised; was someone fighting at the front who had a German grandmother to be hauled out of the line and interned? What about the Royal Family? The king had had a German grandfather, and the queen was wholly German by birth. The absurdity of the hysterical fear of anything German does not seem to have occurred to anyone, or, more likely, if it did, they thought it prudent to remain silent.

The ladies of Falmouth had set up a war hospital supply depot, where they made a wide variety of articles, including bandages, bed jackets, pyjamas, operation stockings, mittens, mufflers, pillows, swabs and dressings. This depot was run from 'Valerie', Woodlane, the house of Mrs. Storer, and by June 1916 they had produced over 7,000 articles. It must have been somewhat daunting for the ladies to be informed that 50,000 pairs of mittens were required for the troops in Mesopotamia by the middle of August, although presumably the War Office was not looking to Falmouth for the entire order.[36] By the end of 1917, the depot was a real hive of industry, producing during that year 15,150 articles of all descriptions for military hospital use in France, Italy, Romania, Aden, Egypt, Mesopotamia and Salonika. Surprisingly, at the annual meeting to consider the year's work, Miss Tweedy found it necessary to complain of 'the slackness of some of the workers',[37] which, considering that they were volunteers and had produced so much, seems a little hard. According to the *Western Morning News*, the town 'had a record of voluntary service which was spoken of with pride' and 'the inhabitants responded well to the calls for patriotic funds'. The work of The Royal Cornwall Sailors' Home was singled out for high praise, in providing shelter, assistance and hospital treatment to seamen of many nationalities stranded in Falmouth as a result of losing their ships due to enemy action. The article acknowledged that, like most towns in time of war, the local authority had to concentrate on maintaining existing services - modernisation and expansion would come later.[38] 1916 was also a record year for Falmouth Hospital, with 146 in-patients, compared with 112 in 1915 and 125 in 1914, of which 126 were surgical. The hospital also dealt with 414 out-patients.[39]

In August 1916, visitors to most Cornish resorts were about up to pre-war numbers. The county was considered to be safe from air raids and naval attack, and people were looking once again to take holidays, a practice which in the early days of the war was considered unpatriotic.[40] However, Falmouth seems to have been the odd town out, as by October, the Chamber of Commerce were concerned about the lack of visitors during the summer season. They had anticipated that visitors would flock to the town to escape the air raids in the east of the country, but they had not done so, instead going to places such as Lynton and Lynmouth. It was thought that this was due in part to insufficient advertising by the town and in part to Falmouth becoming a naval and military centre, whilst people preferred to go to a place for rest and quiet.[41] Another matter which was troubling the Chamber of Commerce concerned neutral liners calling at Falmouth and buying provisions in large quantities, resulting in prices rising steeply for residents. The secretary commented, with considerable candour, that, 'he did not know that Falmouth objected. It was one of the benefits they thought they got from ships calling there'. But another member said, 'The Dutchman sells all he can to the Germans at high prices, and comes here and buys up all he can cheaply'.[42] This was clearly a matter of public concern as there were many letters to the *Packet* on the subject, the vast majority of which were very much against the provisioning of neutral liners, in case the foodstuffs eventually reached Germany. One surprising aspect of this correspondence is that a letter would appear answering points made in another letter - and both letters would appear, one above the other, in the same edition of the paper![43] The *Western Morning News,* in an article on life in Falmouth in 1916, highlighted the problem, which it claimed resulted in 'the inhabitants being almost deprived of certain necessaries of life by the Dutch boats, and having to pay almost famine prices for some articles of food'.[44]

The war had brought an immense increase in shipping visiting the port, as was evidenced by the fact that the medical officer, Dr. J.S.Hicks, reported to the Falmouth & Truro Port Sanitary Authority in September 1916 that during the previous three months '500 vessels of all nationalities have been visited and duly examined by your officers'. Whilst he thought that there was remarkably little disease among seamen, he was very concerned that where there was disease, the medical officer very often was not the first to visit the ship, being preceded by the agents, who might transmit disease from the ship to the townsfolk.[45] Dr. Hicks did not mention the fact in his report but, in addition to the agents, every ship was first visited by an examination officer to ensure that there were no enemy aliens aboard and that the cargo was not intended for an enemy country. The duties of the examination officers will be dealt with in a later chapter.

13th November 1916. 'Ponus' burning on rocks west of Gyllyngase, painting by Rowbotham

The resignation of Asquith as prime minister and the appointment of Lloyd George merited only a small paragraph in the *Packet* of 8th December 1916.[46] However, the war had brought a radical change in attitudes to universal suffrage. As regards men, and even in 1916 there was not universal adult male suffrage, few could see the justice in requiring them to fight but denying them the vote. No woman had the vote in 1916, but the sacrifices made by women together with the huge contribution made by their war work greatly softened attitudes to female suffrage. 'A large body of men now feel that the women - the suffering and busy war-work women - have proved that they would bring fine and valuable qualities to the solution of public questions, and that political life would gain appreciably if women were asked to vote in parliamentary elections'.[47]

Alderman A.W. Chard was elected Mayor for the fifth successive year. In his proposal speech, Councillor A.W. Cox paid tribute to the work which the Mayor had done to cement good relations with the military and naval authorities, 'thousands of men were now stationed in the town, an important naval base was established and the volume of shipping increased considerably, all throwing heavy responsibilities and duties on the municipal authorities and especially on the Mayor and officials'. He went on to say that, once peace had been restored, among the many problems to be solved was 'that of the terribly high death rate among infants and young children. The death rate for infants in Falmouth last year was 153 per 1,000 births. In some of the model cities such as Hampstead and Letchworth the mortality had been reduced to from four to ten per 1,000'. Further problems yet to be tackled were the number of persons living in housing and surroundings not fit for human habitation, the prevalence of venereal disease and 'an apathy and stolid indifference to municipal and public work' on the part of the 'leisured and better educated'.[48]

In early November 1916, an oil tanker, *Ponus*, of 5,077 tons, was driven ashore by a heavy gale at

'Ponus' on fire at Swanpool Point, after having been wrecked

Gyllyngvase beach. Attempts to tow her off failed because of the heavy seas and the lifeboat could not get along side. Two boats were launched from the ship, one reaching land safely but the other overturning in the surf. Watchers on the beach rushed into the surf up to their shoulders and rescued all the seamen struggling in the sea. The lifeboat later managed to get to the ship and took off the rest of the crew apart from the second mate. Fire then broke out in the ship and spread very rapidly, the funnel eventually crashing over the side. 'Seeing the great danger of the second mate, a young army officer, Lieut. E. Badger, and a Mr. Williams rowed out to the ship in a dinghy, by which time the mate had jumped into the sea; they found him, but could not get him into the boat, so tied him to it with a rope and brought him ashore - the man was much exhausted'.[49] This drama resulted in a later High Court action brought by the owners of the *Ponus* against Mr. T.F. Jewell, assistant examination officer at Falmouth, alleging that the ship had been directed to an unsafe anchorage. Mr. Jewell's successful defence was that he did not direct the ship to any particular anchorage, and that it was up to the captain to go where he liked and his duty to keep his weather eye open for change of wind.[50]

NOTES

[1] WB, 17.1.1916, p2
[2] WB, 20.4.1916, p4
[3] WB, 26.3.1916, p7
[4] FP, 31.3.1916
[5] FP, 14.4.1916
[6] WB, 17.4.1916, p2
[7] FP, 20.10.1916, p3
[8] FP, 21.4.1916, p6
[9] FP, 19.5.1916
[10] FP, 9.6.1916, p4
[11] FP, 16.6.1916, p6
[12] FP, 19.5.1916, p2
[13] WB, 4.5.1916, p5
[14] FP, 11.8.1916, p4
[15] Robert K. Massie, *Castles of Steel*, p154
[16] FP, 25.8.1916, p3

[17] FP, 9.5.1919, p5
[18] WB, 8.5.1916, p2
[19] WB, 29.5.1916, p2
[20] WB, 18.9.1916, p1
[21] WB, 18.9.1916, p1
[22] WB, 20.11.1916, p3
[23] FP, 10.5.1916, p4
[24] Reprinted in FP, 28.1.1916, p6
[25] FP, 3.3.1916, p3
[26] FP, 28.4.1916, p5
[27] FP, 15.9.1916, p2
[28] FP, 8.3.1918, p2
[29] FP, 6.10.1916, p4
[30] WB, 20.3.1916, p2
[31] WB, 17.4.1916, p2
[32] WB, 8.5.1916, p2
[33] FP, 23.6.1916, p3

[34] FP, 30.6.1916, p3
[35] FP, 16.6.1916, p6
[36] FP, 21.7.1916, p3
[37] FP, 15.2.1918, p3
[38] *Western Morning News*, reprinted in FP, 5.1.1917, p4
[39] FP, 16.3.1917, p3
[40] WB, 7.8.1916, p2
[41] FP, 6.10.1916, p3
[42] FP, 9.6.1916, p4
[43] FP, 15.12.1916, p3
[44] *Western Morning News*, reprinted in FP, 5.1.1917, p4
[45] FP, 29.9.1916, p4
[46] FP, 18.12.1916, p3
[47] WB, 21.8.1916, p2
[48] FP, 10.11.1916, p3
[49] FP, 10.11.1916, p4
[50] WB, 27.12.1916, p7

CHAPTER IX

'FALMOUTH FOR INSTRUCTIONS' - THE NAVAL BASE

Early in 1915, a Naval Base was established at Falmouth, which had control of all matters relating to the Navy, ships and shipping, patrol boats, the harbour and the bay. A steamer was commandeered to act as a guard boat and the hulks of the Falmouth Coal Company were requisitioned. Search lights were worked from Pendennis Point, St. Mawes castle and St. Anthony Lighthouse and these played on the harbour, the bay and adjoining shores on most nights. Numerous steam trawlers were converted into patrol vessels as were two yachts, the *Venetia* and the *Rovanska*, the latter owned by the famous Marconi. A boom consisting of iron network and supported by barrels at intervals and subsequently superseded by iron chainwork, was stretched across the bay, from St. Anthony Light to Porthallow, outside the Helford River, with an opening at the south end for vessels to enter and leave. At least two steamers managed to collide with the boom and did considerable damage. Inside this, shipping of every description found a safe and commodious anchorage.

As has been seen, from the outbreak of war enemy ships or those from neutral countries suspected of assisting the enemy or breaking the blockade were escorted into Falmouth. The story of one such vessel shows how scrupulously the authorities acted. A Dutch steamer, the *Alwina*, was seized at Falmouth in January 1915, suspected of carrying coal to aid the enemy. She had taken on board at Newport a cargo of coal, ostensibly for carriage to Buenos Aires, although the ship herself did not have nearly enough bunker coal to reach that far destination, and had got as far as Tenerife, where she loitered for over a month. Increasing suspicion that her real intention was to replenish the coal stocks of German raiders forced her captain to sell his cargo to an English firm, and he then returned to Falmouth, where the ship was seized as a neutral vessel carrying contraband intended to benefit enemy warships. The Dutch owner appealed against the confiscation to the Prize Court, which delivered judgement in May 1916. It was held as a fact that the ship had sailed from Newport under false papers with the intention of delivering her cargo of coal to German warships. Had she succeeded in this, she would have been liable to seizure and confiscation. However, in the event, 'the original intention to carry to the enemy had been frustrated and abandoned' and therefore the Court held that she had not been guilty of an offence for which she could be seized, and that the ship must be restored to her owner, although the Court showed its disapproval of the latter by making him liable for all the costs of the proceedings.[1]

The queens of the shipping using Falmouth were the great Dutch liners, carrying passengers and cargoes from America, but these were just as much under the control of the Naval Base as the coal ships. The passengers embarking at Falmouth were examined by an Alien Officer at the Docks, and those intending to disembark were examined on board. Falmouth being designated a 'Defended Port', fishing vessels were not allowed at night to be within ten miles of the harbour. An examination steamer was stationed near the mouth of the harbour; this showed a variety of night and day signals by which it might be recognised and was in communication by Morse code with Pendennis Castle. Any vessel entering or leaving the harbour had to report to the examination steamer and take instructions from her, and if the vessel disobeyed those instructions a shot fired from the Castle across her bows had the desired effect.[2] The Examination Service was set up on the outbreak of war, when the internationally known expression of 'Falmouth for Orders' was amended to 'Falmouth for Instructions', as a host of shipping from all nations were ordered by the Navy to report to Falmouth for examination and instructions how to proceed, if at all. Every ship entering the harbour was visited, inspected and cleared before suppliers and other civilian agencies could make any contact. Each such ship had to fly a particular flag, and the signal that a ship had been cleared was the lowering of this flag.[3] Throughout the war, naval and military officers with foreign language skills closely examined passengers, and their papers and luggage, and if they were uncertain or unsatisfied, sailings could be delayed for days. All mails were removed from liners, carefully censored, and then forwarded to their destinations.

The German Military Attache in New York, Franz von Papen, a future German Chancellor, travelling home via a Dutch liner under a 'safe conduct pass', had a rude shock when he found that all his confidential and secret papers were confiscated by the Examination Officer in Falmouth. 'There is not the slightest doubt that when he was accosted at Falmouth, he was under the false illusion that a 'safe conduct' covered fully not only himself but also all his belongings. The correspondence he carried with him was not hidden away, and some of the letters were in his pockets. When 'detained' he flourished his safe conduct and demanded to be allowed to proceed unmolested on his way. He was politely informed that in the present distressful circumstances of war, a safe conduct applied only to his body corporal and absolutely nothing else. The fact that he would be allowed to proceed on his journey wearing his clothes was entirely due to the grace of the British Navy! Whereupon he used - in the very best English - some extremely uncomplimentary language. In a word, he was extremely angry, and it was with very bad grace indeed that he finally handed over his documents'.[4] These showed that von Papen had been in close contact with a spy, recently executed in the Tower of London.

A Mr. James Archibald, passing as a war correspondent, was arrested when his ship reached Falmouth, and a search of his cabin revealed a letter written by the Austrian ambassador to the United States to his government. This letter stated that the majority of the workers in American steelworks were of Austro-Hungarian extraction and could be persuaded to strike, if the price was right. As the United States was neutral, this caused outrage, and the Austro-Hungarian government was forced to recall their ambassador.[5] Another big fish caught in this manner was Capt. Frans von Rintelen, 'the head of the German spy system in the United States', who was reputed to have £7,000,000 at his disposal to pursue German interests in the States and Mexico.[6] On a separate occasion, six German nationals were taken under armed escort from the liner *Trebantia*, three of whom were doctors.[7]

The most famous of spies to pass through Falmouth was the notorious Mata Hari in 1916. She was on her way to Amsterdam from Spain when the ship in which she was travelling was ordered into Falmouth. She was taken under escort to London, where she was examined by intelligence experts, who were uncertain whether she was a genuine double agent, and decided to return her to Spain, so she was sent back to Falmouth under guard and put on a ship bound for Vigo. The examination officer, E.J. Moseley, who dealt with Mata Hari at Falmouth, wrote that she had much enjoyed her stay in London as she had been put up at the Ritz. Later that year Mata Hari was executed as a spy by the French. Moseley wrote that people engaged in espionage thought up many ways of hiding their dispatches from the examination officers. Secret papers were found on ships 'behind mirrors, cabin wash-ups, under a binnacle compass stand, in ships' boats, and, one occasion, between the drawer and bottom of a bird cage'. On another occasion, a picture was unscrewed from the wall, revealing a small hole in the cabin panelling, and papers were found between this and the skin of the ship.[8] It seems that Falmouth acquired a considerable reputation far and wide as a result of the work of the Examination Service. 'Not long since, an American shipping official remarked to a gentleman connected with a local shipping firm that he was under the impression that Falmouth was a huge city, judging by the notoriety which it enjoyed in America for discovering German and Austrian spies.'[9]

The aerodrome constructed near Bonython on the Helston-Lizard road was home to two airships and several aircraft, which were frequently to be seen flying over the Bay in their search for enemy submarines or minelayers. Two steamers, which had been torpedoed and were making for the safety of the harbour, sank inside the boom, one off Maenporth and the other off the Lighthouse, the latter having a cargo of wheat which as it decayed let off such a putrid smell that fishing boats had to keep to windward. This ship marked its own grave as even at high water, the top of the mast with a flag flying from it was visible. 'Two or three steamers that escaped from sinking owing to the strength of their bulkheads, after having been torpedoed, had holes right through them so that it was like looking through a jagged sort of tunnel. There were several beached near the Bar, which presented the unusual spectacle of big steamers so near the town'.[10]

Once the Naval Base was set up in early 1915, trawlers and net drifters arrived to carry out patrol and anti-submarine work. The drifters were fitted with steel nets which were intended to catch submarines, and they worked inside the trawlers which were armed. These nets were about 200 yards long with a mesh of about 12 feet, and later in the war they were fitted with electrical contact mines at intervals. If this seems bizarre, there is a recorded incident of a trawler, the *Rosetta*, fishing near the Wolf Light, having great difficulty in hauling in her net even with the aid of her steam capstan. Eventually after using the ship's full power, the 'catch' was hauled up - a U-boat, upon which the trawler opened fire at close range and the submarine disappeared, presumed sunk. Whether any of the drifters with their special steel nets ever 'bagged' a U-boat is not known to the author. The trawlers and drifters were also used extensively for mine sweeping purposes, as huge numbers of mines were laid by the enemy in the approaches to Falmouth, and at least one trawler, the *St. Ives*, was lost with most of her crew on mine sweeping duties.[11] However, despite the dangers inherent in their work, there were comparatively few losses of men or ships among the Falmouth based minesweepers, which is surprising considering that 1000 men lost their lives in British minesweepers in the war.

The *Packet* always used a not very subtle distinction between German and British submarines, referring to the former as 'pirates', and the latter as 'HM Submarines'. What is described as 'the Pirates' Ruse' was the use of sails on U-boats to disguise them.[12] Another ploy of U-boats was to make use of an accompanying merchant ship as a decoy, behind which the sub would hide and then come out and sink its prey. This happened to a British merchantman off Pendeen.[13] Under the heading 'The Revival of Piracy', the *Packet* compared German submarines to the pirates, thieves and murderers of Elizabethan times. 'The recent accomplishments of the sea exponents of 'frightfulness' should shame into silence even the most obstinate member of the little band of 'friends of Germany' in our midst'.[14] However, under the heading 'A Gentle Pirate', the *Briton* did acknowledge that the captain of the U29 'did his unpleasant business in a most pleasant way'. It appears that the captain invited aboard the captains of merchant ships which he had sunk for cigars and a bottle of wine, before towing the boats containing the crews towards safety - 'the crews were treated as considerately as was consistent with the attempted destruction of their vessels'.[15] The fate of the unarmed Falmouth schooner *Fortuna* was typical of many. Homeward bound from Le Havre with a cargo of scrap iron, she was stopped by a German submarine, and the crew were given five minutes to abandon ship, and were then summoned alongside the submarine and compelled to give the name and description of their vessel, the nature of her cargo and where she was bound. The crew had to give up one of their boats so that the Germans could go across to the *Fortuna* and place explosive charges on her, having first removed all brass and copper. The ship was then sunk, the U-boat departed and the crew were eventually rescued by a passing steamer and taken to Plymouth.[16]

Thus, the most difficult question facing the Royal Navy was, how best to deal with the U-boat menace. Steel nets could not be the answer, nor could even more quixotic methods. One of these was to send out motor launches carrying two swimmers, one armed with a black bag, the other with a hammer. If a periscope was sighted, the launch was to come as close as possible. Then the swimmers were to dive in, one would attempt to place his black bag over the periscope, and, if he failed, the other would try to smash the glass with his hammer. Another scheme, not blessed with success, involved attempting to teach seagulls to defecate on periscopes.[17] Considerably more successful were the 'Q' ships, innocent looking schooners and small steamers which had been converted so that within thirty seconds their disguise could be removed and their guns brought into action. The most famous of these, indeed the most famous ship to be based at Falmouth, was the *Mary B. Mitchell*, who deserves, and will receive, a chapter to herself. But the vital innovation to combat the U-boat, introduced only when the unseen enemy threatened to bring the nation to its knees in 1917, was the introduction of the convoy system.

Falmouth Bay became the collection point for convoys; sometimes over a hundred vessels were formed into a convoy, and it was said that they presented 'an impressive though somewhat motley appearance; the steamers strangely camouflaged in many varieties of pattern; other craft often largely composed of smallish yawls and cutters generally laden with coal for the continent'.[18] A large number of steamers would gather in the Bay each week to be formed into a convoy to the Mediterranean, which left under destroyer escort every eight days, and although the convoy system greatly reduced the number of ships sunk, the U-boats attacked incessantly and on one occasion, on the 26th December 1917, the last two ships in the convoy, *Tregenna* and *Benito*, were torpedoed some 14 miles after weighing anchor in the Bay. The former sank within 13 minutes; the latter survived the first attack but was helpless on a moonlit night with only an armed trawler for protection, and 13 hours later the U-boat returned and torpedoed her again, this time sinking her. Questions were raised in Parliament, from which it appeared that tugs had been dispatched to find the stricken vessel but for some reason could not find her, itself the subject of a further enquiry.[19]

In addition, there was the weekly French convoy, 'a most interesting sight, as every sailing ship that was possible to fill with coal was requisitioned, yachts, fishing boats, schooners and various other craft, and on the 3rd August 1917, 123 craft left the port, stretching away across the Channel in line for many miles'.[20] Until the convoy system was introduced in June 1917, 10% of merchant shipping was sunk by U-boats; thereafter this was drastically reduced to 1%. 58 convoys assembled at Falmouth, carrying 3½ million tons of cargo, and only 6 vessels were lost. These figures referred only to ocean convoys. In addition there was the coastal trade, which was so enormous that it is difficult to give figures'. There was a huge coal trade with France, and the ships would come down from Bristol and the South Wales ports, be made up into convoys at Penzance and Falmouth, and sent across to France, the vessels returning with iron ore. About ten million tons of coal were shipped in this manner, and six million tons of iron ore brought back, and the number of ships escorted in convoys exceeded 12,000. 'The vessels employed in this trade being small, an enormous number of them had been employed. Yet we had only lost 35 of them from enemy causes'.[21] At the Peace Celebrations in July 1919, Commander Collett, the second-in-command at the Naval Base, gave some telling statistics and details of the work carried out there. 'Patrolling and minesweeping was very monotonous work. It was carried on week after week without perhaps even seeing a submarine, and when the men came back for a rest, it was very nice for them to feel that they were among friends'. They had to patrol the coast from Looe to Hartland Point and to carry out minesweeping in the same area. There had been about 120 engagements with enemy submarines, destroying 8, officially damaging 5 others, and damaging many others which could not be officially confirmed. 292 mines had been swept, 858 big steamers convoyed out into the Atlantic and only 6 torpedoed, 2,127 sailing ships with coal had been escorted to France, 5,163 steamers similarly escorted from Mount's Bay, and 5,442 steamers escorted back from France, making a total of 10,605 steamers, only 35 of which had been lost. 29 steamers had been salvaged and brought into Falmouth for repair, and the patrol boats had saved the lives of 600 seamen whose ships had been sunk.[22]

Wartime always brings forth a rich crop of bizarre stories. Dr. James Whetter in *The History of Falmouth* writes:
'Another story relating to subs illustrates the rather casual character of the war in its early stages. Some sailors belonging to a German sub, it is said, brought their vessel right close to the shore. They landed on a beach near Pendennis, and went into Falmouth to the cinema. Unrecognised for what they were, they later returned to the sub and put to sea again'.[23]

Another story, which cannot be vouched for, is that a naval vessel was operating in the Irish Sea when the officer of the watch distinctly heard what sounded like the ringing of a telephone. He sent away a boat, and the officer in charge came across a box on the surface of the water from which the ringing emitted. Opening the box, the officer found a telephone. He picked up the receiver, said 'Hello', and was astounded to hear a man's voice tell him that he was connected to a British submarine resting on the sea bottom.[24] The origin of this story may well be the fact that in 1915, one ingenious anti-U-boat method consisted of a trawler moving slowly at sea, apparently on innocent business. From the stern of the trawler dropped two lines, one a tow cable and the other a telephone wire, which were attached to a submerged submarine. If a U-boat was tempted to attack the trawler, the latter would inform the submarine by telephone, which would cast off the tow and attempt to torpedo the U-boat, and indeed at least two U-boats were sunk in this way.[25]

In late 1916, the 'sink at sight' policy of the German government caused several Dutch steamers to seek refuge at Falmouth, and they were ordered to go up to moor in the Truro River. As the owners were anxious to get their ships and cargoes to Holland, negotiations took place between the Dutch and German authorities, and agreement was reached for seven ships to proceed to Dutch ports, subject to three conditions. The ships had to be painted from stem to stern in the colours, black, white and red, of the German Mercantile Marine, they had to follow a specified route and, lastly, they had to leave on a specified date. These conditions were complied with, and on 22nd February 1917, seven Dutch steamers, totalling 36,000 tons, left Falmouth for Holland, sailing under the direct instructions of the Dutch government, with navigation and other lights clearly illuminating the vessels. Notwithstanding the agreement reached between the two governments, the seven ships were stopped by a German U-boat, the crew of which placed explosives in the engine rooms of each ship, sinking six of them and badly damaging the seventh, which however was able to make her way back to Falmouth and was repaired.[26] Holland was a neutral country, and the ships were sailing under a German guarantee of 'relative security'. As *Punch* ironically put it, 'Germany is so often misunderstood. It should be obvious by this time that her attitude to International Law has always been one of approximate reverence'.[27] 300 crew members from the Dutch ships were rescued by trawlers and landed at Falmouth.[28]

The Base was first commanded by Captain V.E.B. Phillimore, then by Rear Admiral Dennison and, in the last two years of the war, by Rear Admiral J.S. Luard, with Commander Collett as his second-in-command, and having their headquarters at 'Penwennack' on Bar Road. Luard's previous appointment had been second-in-command of the Northern Patrol whose task it was to maintain the blockade of Germany by intercepting and, if necessary, directing to British ports any ship of a neutral country which might be carrying cargoes of use to Germany.[29] However, it does appear that Luard slightly blotted his copybook when, on the Northern Patrol, he allowed a ship claiming to be the Dutch vessel *Gamma* to proceed although she was some 150 miles to the westward of the track prescribed for Dutch vessels; it transpired that the ship in question was in fact a German supply ship assisting a raider in the Atlantic, and a Court of Enquiry was held into the incident. The Admiralty were content merely 'to request that Commodore John Luard may be informed that he ought not to have allowed the ship to pass without making further enquiries as to why a ship from Holland to Falmouth was some 150 miles to the westward of the track prescribed'.[30] Luard was posted to Falmouth immediately after this episode in March 1917, as Senior Naval Officer and as a Rear Admiral on the retired list. In June 1918, he was made a Companion of the Most Honourable Order of the Bath.[31]

At the end of the war, Admiral Luard said that the Falmouth based minesweepers would continue with their work despite the Armistice, as it would be necessary to sweep the coasts for a depth of ten miles to clear as many mines as possible, and all fishermen would have to be aware of the danger from mines for many years to come.[32] Twelve of the mine sweeping trawlers based at Falmouth were then sold to the American Navy, which had undertaken some minesweeping duties in the North Sea.[33]

Admiral Luard's flag, as commander of the Naval Base, was hauled down for the last time in August 1919. Some minesweepers remained for a few months, but the base was finally closed down in December 1919.[34] There was foreboding in Falmouth that the Admiralty intended to sever connections permanently with the Fal - 'it can scarcely be imagined that the Government can afford to neglect a place which has proved of such vast value to the nation during the War, and yet strange things do happen'. There was every reason for such foreboding. Throughout the war the civic authorities had lobbied the Admiralty and the government to develop Falmouth both as a naval and a mercantile port. In June 1917, the Chamber of Commerce passed a resolution drawing the government's attention to 'the importance in the present crisis of using to the utmost extent the natural facilities offered at the port of Falmouth for the discharge of cargoes essential to the national interest, it being obvious such cargoes which reach Falmouth should be discharged there during the present submarine activity, and not be sent to sea again to the other ports and run the risk of total loss'.[35] A delegation from the Town Council, the Chamber of Commerce and the Docks Company had discussions with the Admiralty, and hopes were high that the port would be developed by the government, but such hopes were doomed to disappointment. A councillor, Mr. W.C. Bullen, was entirely correct when, on the return of the delegation in optimistic mood, he said that Plymouth was a formidable rival.[36] For hundreds of years Plymouth had been the main westerly naval base, and it was extremely unlikely that there would ever be the public money to develop both Plymouth and Falmouth, so if the Admiralty had to choose between them, Plymouth had more than a head start. It was noted with alarm that on the first peacetime cruise of the Atlantic fleet, ships would visit Torbay and Penzance, but not Falmouth.[37] Subsequent protests to the Admiralty from the Mayor and Comrades of the Great War, the forerunner of the Royal British Legion, resulted in the cruiser *Castor* and four destroyers visiting Falmouth in September 1919.[38] Interestingly, this is somewhat at odds with a report in the *Briton* which stated that a much more impressive force visited Falmouth, and then Penzance - the battleships *Barham*, *Valiant* and *Warspite*[39] - but the *Packet*, being on the spot, is more likely to be accurate in its report.

The *Western Morning News* described Falmouth as,
'The principal war zone of the county, both military and naval. Its importance as the first and last port has been fully demonstrated during the last four and a half years, and there has been very great activity both in relation to ordinary shipping and naval operations... . The harbour dues were never so great, the pilots and boatmen enjoyed a most lucrative time, and the tradesmen also reaped a good harvest from the unprecedented conditions... . Many enemy aliens who were endeavouring to return to their respective countries were arrested and interned, and a few important spies were captured... . The bay was a rendezvous for vessels awaiting convoy, and daily after the inauguration of the convoy system, the waters off Gyllyngvase held large numbers of ships. Very few places had the peril of the submarine menace more strikingly brought home to them. Thousands of seamen whose vessels had been torpedoed were landed at the port, and many vessels which had been severely damaged by the Hun pirate were towed into the harbour in view of the inhabitants, and were beached and repaired. When the enemy submarine warfare was at its height, hundreds of rescued seamen were in a week

A battle squadron anchored in Falmouth Bay during the war

Battle Fleet in Falmouth Bay

landed and cared for. One night, for instance, 150 men were brought ashore, and as many as three crews in one day. In connection with these, the Royal Cornwall Sailors' Home and the British and Foreign Sailors' Society did splendid work. Over and over again the Home was crowded out with these unfortunate men, and the surplus had to be accommodated in hotels and lodging houses'.[40]

Hospital Ship in Falmouth Harbour (with Quay Punt)

British submarines in Falmouth Docks during the war

A special tribute should be paid to the work of the Royal Cornwall Sailors' Home & Hospital, which, during the war, treated 641 patients from naval patrol vessels and minesweepers, necessitating the provision of an extra ward, and an enlarged nursing staff. The Hospital also treated 441 men from the mercantile marine, including many injured in U-boat attacks. 'Between 200 and 300 crews, or portions thereof, numbering nearly 3,000 men were fed, lodged and provided with comforts by the Institution, and altogether the record does honour to the port and even to the nation'.[41] No other port in the UK approached the record of Falmouth in providing for the needs of men who had been torpedoed. Founded in 1852, the hospital had 19 beds in 1914, but by the end of the war these had been increased to 34.[42] Its existence depended on voluntary subscriptions, and among these was a paltry fifteen guineas a year from the Admiralty, which as the Mayor pointed out in 1917 was nothing short of a scandal. In fact, as His Worship stated, despite the magnificent work done at the Home for the seamen of the Empire, only one hundred guineas a year was obtained in subscriptions from the Empire. Considering that shipwrecked merchant seamen were boarded and lodged free, provided with fresh clothing and had their railway fares paid for them to their home towns, the support of the shipowners was niggardly. However, the support, or lack of it, from the Admiralty was even worse because, as the chairman, Sir Arthur Vivian, pointed out, three quarters of the patients in the hospital were Royal Naval personnel, and indeed it could be argued in time of total war that the whole of the merchant service also formed part of the Navy.[43]

Whilst the powers-that-be were fulsome in their praise of those who had served in the Navy, the war gratuity which they received was graduated according to rank, with the most senior non-commissioned officers getting the maximum of £36. Even this was not paid to them in cash, but a Post Office Savings Account was compulsorily opened in the name of each recipient and the gratuity was credited to that account, the pass book for which was handed to each sailor as he was demobilised.[44]

NOTES

[1] WB, 8.5.1916, p2
[2] W. Lloyd Fox, ibid
[3] WB, 17.2.1916, p7
[4] FP, 21.1.1916, p5
[5] WB, 9.9.1915, p4
[6] FP, 17.12.1915, p4
[7] FP, 24.12.1915, p4
[8] E. J. Moseley, ibid
[9] FP, 30.5.1919, p6
[10] W. Lloyd Fox, ibid
[11] E. J. Moseley, ibid
[12] FP, 4.6.1915, p2
[13] FP, 18.6.1915, p2
[14] FP, 2.4.1915, p2
[15] WB, 25.3.1915, p4
[16] WB, 7.8.1916, p2
[17] Robert K. Massie, Castles of Steel, p525
[18] W. Lloyd Fox, 'Falmouth and the Great War, presidential address to the Royal Cornwall Polytechnic Society, undated but possibly 1924
[19] FP, 18.1.1918, p3
[20] E.J. Moseley, 'Mine and Anti-Submarine Operations carried out during the War, off the Cornish Coast', Royal Cornwall Polytechnic Society, undated
[21] Admiral Thursby, C-in-C Plymouth, reported in FP, 20.12.1918, p3
[22] FP, 25.7.1919, p3
[23] Dr. James Whetter, The History of Falmouth, p70
[24] Dr. E.J. Williams in a letter to the author dated January 2004
[25] Robert K. Massie, Castles of Steel, p718
[26] WB, 26.12.1917, p2 and E.J. Moseley, ibid
[27] Mr. Punch's History of the Great War, p140
[28] FP, 2.3.1917
[29] Grainger, ibid., p648
[30] Grainger, ibid., p668
[31] FP, 7.6.1918, p3
[32] FP, 29.11.1918
[33] FP, 23.5.1919, p5
[34] FP, 5.12.1919, p4
[35] WB, 7.6.1917, p5
[36] WB, 21.6.1917, p7
[37] FP, 15.8.1919, p5
[38] FP, 19.9.1919, p3
[39] WB, 25.9.1919, p3
[40] WMN, 29.12.1918
[41] FP, 21.3.1919, p2
[42] FP, 23.5.1919, p3
[43] WB, 7.5.1917, p3
[44] WB, 2.1.1919, p2

CHAPTER X

THE *MARY B.*

In April 1916, a sailing ship, the *Mary B. Mitchell*, 227 tons and built in 1892, called at Falmouth on her way to a Welsh port, and was requisitioned, at a hire charge of £60 a month, so that she could be fitted out as a decoy vessel or 'Q' ship. She was officially renamed H.M.S. *Mitchell*, or Q9, but was always known at the Falmouth Base as the *MBM*. She was armed with a 12 pounder, hidden behind a dummy deckhouse, and two six pounders under hatches and all mounted on swinging pedestals, together with Lewis guns, grenades and small arms. All these armaments were hidden, so that to an enemy vessel she was an unarmed sailing merchantman, but her disguise could be thrown off and every gun brought into action within thirty seconds. It has to be remembered that in the Great War, submarines were still comparatively in their infancy, and their captains much preferred to attack either with gun or torpedo on the surface, rather than submerged. The idea behind the Q ships was that they, as apparently helpless merchantmen, would lure an unsuspecting U-boat into an attack on the surface; the Q ship would then drop her disguise and hope to destroy the U-boat before it could dive. The first German ship to be brought into Falmouth as a prize in 1914 was the three masted schooner *Else*. She was renamed *Prize*, converted into a Q ship, and her captain, Lieut. W.A. Sanders, won the VC in a battle with U93.[1] If the *MBM* was not the first Q ship, she was to become renowned far beyond Falmouth for her exploits. She was manned by volunteers, all members of the Royal Naval Reserve and two being over 60; her first captain was Lieut. M. Armstrong DSO, who moved to another ship in early 1917, and Lieut. John Lawrie DSO, DSC (with Bar) was promoted from navigating officer to take command.

Her usual crew, when trading in peace time, was the master, the mate and about six seamen, and the accommodation was both luxurious and ample because not only was she used to carry slate from Welsh ports to the continent and to return with other cargoes, but also she acted as the private yacht of her owner, Lord Penrhyn, who made summer trips in her to the Mediterranean. As a 'Q' ship her complement was three officers and about eighteen ratings. This made for very cramped conditions on board and gymnastic apparatus and boxing gloves were provided to keep the men fit during periods of inactivity. Between patrols all stayed ashore in or near Falmouth. There was also a dog, Torps, and three ship's cats. She sailed under several disguises such as the Spanish *Mary Y Jose* of Vigo, the French *Marie Therese* of Cette and *Jeanette* of La Houle, and the Russian *Neptune* of Riga. All these were of similar size, but mostly constructed in wood, whilst the *MBM* was of steel construction.[2]

Returning to Falmouth after her first four week patrol, she so deceived the Falmouth patrol vessels that they boarded this 'Spanish' schooner and needed a lot of convincing as to her *bona fides*.[3] On 20th June 1917, the *MBM* encountered three U-boats in one day. One ruse used, on sighting a U-boat, was to send away a boat, known as 'the panic party', to give the impression of abandoning ship and thereby to lure the submarine nearer, so, on sighting a U-boat about 3 miles away, the panic party was sent away. The U-boat opened fire, but the *MBM* held her fire until the enemy was about 850 yards distant, and then got off 17 rounds, apparently scoring seven hits. The submarine ceased firing and disappeared, leaving an oily slick on the surface of the sea. The whole action had taken two hours. That evening, another U-boat attacked on the surface, and again the panic party was sent away. At this the submarine made straight for the *MBM*, dived and began to surface again only 50

'Mary B Mitchell' as a 'Q' ship - note the 12-pounder near the stern

yards away. 'When a couple of feet of hull was showing, the *Mitchell* opened up with a 6-pounder and a large blue flash and yellow vapour came from a hole in the conning tower. Then the 12-pounder hit the submarine forward and she disappeared in a cloud of black smoke, steam and spray only 25 yards off the *Mitchell's* port bow. The panic party was no sooner on board just after 8.00pm when a third submarine was sighted about five miles astern. She did not attack, was lost to sight and disappeared at dark'.[4]

The panic party was used again on 3rd August 1917 when another U-boat gradually approached, shelling all the time. The skipper of the *MBM* held his nerve as shells burst through sails and rigging, until the U-boat was only 1000 yards away, then cleared the guns for action and got away about 20 rounds, three or four of which appeared to hit the base of the conning tower. The U-boat then dived and was seen no more, having wasted over 70 shells. Two men were injured on the *MBM*, which suffered damage to the windlass, sails, rigging and deck fittings. The unfortunate 'panic party' found themselves between the *MBM* and the U-boat during this action, and one shell burst about ten feet from the boat, taking off an officer's cap and filling the boat with water.[5]

Another encounter with a U-boat took place on 19th December 1917 off Trevose Head, when the submarine was damaged but got away. The success of the *MBM* in damaging and driving off U-boats, if not necessarily destroying them,[6] paved the way for other sailing ships to be sent to Falmouth to be similarly fitted out. In her various actions, over 200 shells were fired at the *MBM* by U-boats, some passing through the sails and rigging, but only one hit the hull, fortunately striking the centre of the windlass, otherwise it would have gone right through the bottom of the ship.[7]

An extract from the log kept by the mate, J. Manley, dramatically describes an action on 2nd December 1916:

'Mary B Mitchell', after she had returned to trading in peacetime delivering coal to Falmouth gasworks

'It was 10.00am in the English Channel when, about fifteen miles south of the Wolf Lighthouse, the lookout aloft reported a submarine three points off the starboard bow, towing two lifeboats. Our Commander ordered the guns' crews to stand by for action. At this time we were armed with one 12 pounder, two 6 pounders and a maxim gun, and were without auxiliary propelling power. We allowed the submarine to approach to within 100 yards. Fritz hoisted signals and shouted through his megaphone to abandon ship immediately as he was about to sink us. Orders given for five hands to remain on deck to back the yards and to heave to, the remainder of the ship's company to conceal under the hatchways in readiness for action. The action bell rings, the hatches fall off, the ship's sides fall away and we get in four direct hits on U26. A heavy explosion occurred and the U26 blew up, disappearing as she took her last dive head first. Just as the action finished a second enemy

Three-masted topsail 'Mary B. Mitchell', built at Carrickfergus in 1892 and wrecked near Kirtcudbright, Solway Firth, in 1944. From an original painting by Ieuan Williams, B.A.

submarine with whom the U26 was working, came to the surface and fired a torpedo across our stern, not being able to manoeuvre with only plain sail. Fritz disappeared and we got the two lifeboats alongside, which we found contained a crew of 22 men from a torpedoed Norwegian steamer. The crew gave us a rousing cheer and said that our's was a funny cargo ship. They were taken on board a trawler and landed at Penzance. We then made for Scilly Isles - St. Mary's, where we again disguised our rig'.[8]

Eighteen members of the officers and crew of the *MBM* received decorations for their bravery in the ship's various actions. The mate, Mr. J. Manley, DSM and bar, wrote:

'Our little ship has had marvellous luck in her Royal Naval career as a decoy ship, being dismasted in February 1917, and rescued from a heavy N.W. gale ten miles off Ushant and towed into Brest. After the Armistice, she proceeded to Falmouth and on the 6th December was opened for public exhibition and to boom War Bonds. On the first day £16,000 were received, while the proceeds of the eight days amounted to £36,000. Now her work done, the good old *Mary B. Mitchell* is back at her peaceful occupation. She is a great little ship and will always have a place in the recollections of those privileged and proud to serve upon her'.[9]

When peace returned, the *Mary B* resumed her trading career, carrying coal, pit props, burnt ore and china clay. In the 1930s she was also used as the chief prop in two films, *The Mystery of The Mary Celeste* and *McGluskey the Sea Rover*. In the Second World War, she was chartered for the Lisbon run by Irish shipowners, making five trips carrying coal to Lisbon and returning with other cargoes. Her end came on 14th December 1944, when she was wrecked in the Eden estuary, near Torres Point in Kirkcudbright Bay, in a storm.

'The gallant little vessel had seen exciting times during her 52 years; she was the pride of her builder, she was the pride of the Anglesey slate schooners, her war record was outstanding, the Falmouth people refer to her as 'the Falmouth Mystery Ship', she was the pride of the Arklow schooners and thousands of people knowing nothing of her history must have seen her on film'.[10]

NOTES

[1] E. Keble Chatterton, *Beating The U-Boats*, pp52-55
[2] J.J. Lawrie, The Story of the Mary B. Mitchell, pp6-16
[3] E. Keble Chatterton, ibid., p13
[4] J.J. Lawrie, ibid.
[5] J.J. Lawrie, ibid.
[6] Letter dated 21.6.2000 from Mr. Les Mitchell to Mr. Peter Gilson, with copies attached of U-boat reports to the German Admiralty
[7] FP, 16.12.1918, p4
[8] J. Manley, *Log of HMS Mary B. Mitchell*
[9] J. Manley, ibid.
[10] J.J. Laurie, ibid.

CHAPTER XI

THE GARRISON TOWN

It is impossible to overestimate the effect of the war on the lives of the townsfolk. Not only did the young men go off to fight, and many came home shattered in body or mind, or did not come home at all, but also a peaceful holiday resort became a fortified army camp, garrisoned by up to 14,000 soldiers at any one time, thereby doubling the population. When war was declared, a Garrison Commander, a Colonel, was appointed and Falmouth became a 'defended port'. Bridges, the water works and reservoirs were protected by military guards. Falmouth became 'a prohibited area for the residence of aliens', so did not share in the housing of the many thousands of Belgian refugees. Many horses from Falmouth were commandeered and the golf course was taken over by the Army and Trevethan Camp built there to accommodate the hundreds of men in training. A fort was constructed on the high ground with machine gun emplacements, and covered passages, surrounded with barbed wire entanglements and protecting trenches, to guard the approaches to Falmouth in that direction. Camps were also established at St. Anthony, on the Hornworks and in the Castle grounds, in which many thousands of men were trained. Sentries were placed to prevent anyone approaching the various camps and the Castle Drive was closed to the public. Troops were quartered throughout the town in all possible empty houses and billeted in others. Some officers were accommodated in private houses, but they had the considerable advantage of enjoying 'what must have been the best officer's mess in the entire army', because the entire catering staff of the National Liberal Club in London volunteered, and were posted to Falmouth.[1]

Several companies of Territorial Royal Engineers and Royal Garrison Artillery were raised, and many men joined the DCLI, the Royal Fusiliers, the West Yorks, the Rifle Brigade, the Royal Garrison Artillery, the Royal Engineers, the Army Service Corps, and other units temporarily stationed in Falmouth. Bayonet practice took place in Arwenack Avenue and the Castle Drive, among other places. A rifle range was erected on Pennance Point, where its exposed position caused the butts to suffer more from the high winds than from the accuracy of the firing. Some troops were trained in Mawnan parish, where a rifle range was made on Rosemullion Point. Anticipating the possibility of a raid from the sea at Swanpool, trenches were dug on the west side of Hangman's Hill and a machine gun emplacement was made near the rocket apparatus post at its foot on the east side. The railway line almost as far as Penryn was defended by trenches and machine gun emplacements. A Volunteer Training Corps was formed, but no man between the ages of 19 and 38 could join unless he had been rejected on medical grounds for military service.

In July 1916, the district within five miles of the coast was declared to be a 'prohibited area' and all sketching and photography was forbidden unless prior consent had been obtained by the police, and no such consent could be obtained within the Garrison Command of Falmouth.

Various agencies looked after the welfare of the troops, including the Red Cross, the Voluntary Aid Detachment, and St. John Ambulance Brigade, and the town supported various funds such as The Prisoner of War Fund, the Convalescent Soldiers Fund, and the The Food Depot for Sick and Wounded Soldiers, which operated on Saturdays at the Market House to receive gifts of eggs, fruit, cakes etc. for soldiers in local hospitals.[2]

Practically all the schools were commandeered for use as military hospitals, and the children were taught in the Reading Room at the Free Library, Town Hall, Science and Art Room, Municipal Buildings, Congregational, Wesley, Baptist and Pike's Hill schoolrooms, Earle's Retreat and the Friends' Meeting House. The first contingent of American soldiers to reach this country landed at Falmouth.[3] The great number of soldiers stationed in and around Falmouth enabled cricket, rugby and football leagues to be organised, in which teams from five regiments took part. The first Garrison Cup Cricket League, for which a handsome silver cup, raised by public subscription, was presented, was won by the 4th Battalion West Yorkshire Regiment.[4] The traditional rivalry between Cornwall and Devon was continued on rugby 'fields' at the front in France between teams representing Cornish and Devon regiments. Jack Solomon, of the Redruth club, wrote home, 'whilst the match is in progress, you take no notice of the roar of the cannon and think that you are only out here for the game'.[5]

With many thousands of soldiers and sailors thronging the town, there was bound to be drunkenness and petty crime, and the local magistrates were kept fully occupied. However one very serious crime showed the astonishing speed at which the wheels of justice turned. A soldier was accused of the murder of his girl friend in Penryn on 14th. January 1918. He was brought before the justices on the 15th, and committed for trial at Bodmin Assizes, where his case was heard on 28th January. He was convicted that day and sentenced to death. The sentence was commuted to life imprisonment on 16th February.

Following the Armistice in November 1918, it was natural that men under training would not look at their service in the same light as before. Early in the following January, the 25th Battalion Rifle Brigade, stationed at Trevethan Camp, 600 strong, refused to parade because they were being required to do more drill than at other camps. A deputation from the men went to see the colonel, 'the result was that a promise was made that things shall be put right'.[6] The colonel was

Trevethan Camp, built on the fields west of the Beacon, on the original golf coarse.
'Rosslyn' in the background (now site of Mayfield, Fairfield and Highfield Roads)

immediately replaced.[7]   This was by no means an isolated incident, and indeed was far less serious than many throughout the country. Now that the war was over, men had only one thought - to get home and to take up their 'ordinary' lives again as best they could - and the exasperating slowness of demobilisation led to incidents, up to and including mutiny, which forced the new Secretary of State for War, Winston Churchill, to speed up the return to civilian life.

Militarily, Falmouth played an important part throughout the war, both as a training ground and as a 'defended port' requiring a substantial garrison. It seems rather a poor recognition of this, when, after all the soldiers had marched away, the Corporation were refused consent to take over the living accommodation at Trevethan Camp as 'temporary dwellings for the working classes'. Instead, all the buildings were sold by auction in November 1919.

NOTES

[1] *Guardian*, 8.11.2001, p3
[2] Above 4 paragraphs, W. Lloyd Fox, presidential address to the Royal Cornwall Polytechnic Society, undated but possibly 1922
[3] WMN, 25.12.1918

[4] FP, 8.10.1915, p4
[5] WB, 20.5.1915, p7
[6] FP, 10.1.1919, p3
[7] FP, 31.1.1919, p3

CHAPTER XII

BELT TIGHTENING - 1917

The bleak dawn of yet another year of war was epitomised by the withdrawal from service of that echo of peace time and holidays, the Cornish Riviera, described as the longest non-stop express in the world. Its substitute left Penzance at 9.45am, arriving Paddington at 5.30pm. In the opposite direction, it left Paddington at 10.15am, arriving at Penzance at 6.00pm.[1] Presumably, wartime exigencies caused train journeys to take longer. The *West Briton*, never short of something to complain about, had the railway in its sights for not making sufficiently drastic reductions in its services to meet wartime requirements. Describing the number of trains as 'wasteful' , it was pointed out that on a weekday there were eight trains to and from Truro and Falmouth. This was much the same as before the war and 'no stranger would think...that we are in the midst of a war which is taxing our manpower and our economic strength to the uttermost'. The railways had come under Government control, and so the 'wasteful' service could not be blamed on competition between the railway companies, but 'when it comes to saving money, the authorities display timidity and weakness'.[2]

The importance which Falmouth had achieved as a liner port was shown when, in February 1917, the Germans issued orders to their U-boats, modifying their 'sink on sight' policy, that regular American passenger steamers were to go unmolested, provided:

a   Falmouth was the port of destination
b   The liners bear special signs to identify them
c   One steamer runs in each direction every week, arriving Falmouth on Sundays and leaving Falmouth on Wednesdays.[3]

This was hardly more than a token gesture intended to keep America neutral, but its effect was to infuriate the very people it was meant to placate, and in April 1917 the United States entered the war.

The substantial increase in shipping using the port was evidenced by the report of the Sanitary Inspector of Falmouth and Truro Port Sanitary Authority, which revealed that in 1917 he had inspected 390 British and 270 foreign vessels, and had found very little sickness.[4] In 1916, 956 vessels, in total 132,043 tons, entered the eastern side of the docks, 'no record being available of vessels to and from the western side'.[5] By June 1917, the Harbour Commissioners were reporting a record number of vessels using the harbour, there being between 30 and 40 at any one time.[6]

Whilst the motor car was well established by 1914, horse power in the literal sense was still the preferred method of transport in rural areas, and petrol shortage due to the war only served to increase the importance of the horse and donkey. The Falmouth branch of the Farmers' Union drew the attention of the licensing justices to the ancient requirement of the law for landlords to provide accommodation for man and beast. They pointed out that there was only one licensed house in Falmouth, apart from the Greenbank which was too far out of the town, which provided stabling accommodation. All the others had enlarged their drinking and eating areas at the expense of stabling and 'there was not a town in Cornwall where stabling accommodation was so small as at Falmouth'.[7]

The hard pressed Guardians of the Falmouth Union were criticised for purchasing eleven dozen eggs, which, it was said, should be used for invalids only. Ratepayers could not afford to provide eggs for workhouse inmates, when eggs are needed for soldiers in hospital. In their defence, the Guardians pointed out that the eggs were in part the rations of the officers, and as to the rest were used in the workhouse infirmary.[8] There was further criticism when the Guardians disposed of a donkey, which had served the Board for 30 years, and replaced it with a pony, and yet more complaints about the amount of milk drunk by the fourteen children in the workhouse, six gallons a week, and the amount of sugar consumed by them, 9lb a week, it being claimed that this was more than any other working class children in Falmouth were getting.[9] If this criticism seems on face value rather mean minded, it must be remembered that in 1917 food shortages as a result of the U-boat campaign were biting hard. In April, the Guardians decided that they must halve the rations of bread served at each meal, and to replace this with oatmeal. There was anxious discussion as to what was to happen if the inmates did not like oatmeal - 'in wartime it is not a question of not liking a thing, but we have to eat it'. When a member asked if the inmates could have sugar with the oatmeal, he was told that salt would be served.[10] This measure reduced bread consumption at the Union by one quarter as compared with pre-war levels, so that now each inmate on average was consuming 4lbs 10oz of bread each week.[11] This reduction was in line with the exhortation of the King to the country at large, to reduce bread consumption by one quarter. [12]

With four military hospitals in the town, the sight of sick, wounded and convalescent soldiers was common. However, the unusual case of a private in the DCLI who was wounded and partially paralysed, and had to use crutches to get about, received publicity. He was discharged from the army and took lodgings in Falmouth. Walking along the street on his crutches, he was hit a glancing blow by a taxi and thrown to the ground. 'On endeavouring to get up, he felt a 'click' in his back and immediately received an agreeable surprise'. He found that he could walk normally again, threw away his crutches and re-enlisted.[13]

It was cold enough to skate on Swanpool in February, which was unfortunate for Dr.D.H. Trail, who slipped and broke his ankle.[14] With so many servicemen in the town, the cinema was a good place to escape the cold and was doing excellent business. In addition to the Kozey Picture Palace, the St. George's Hall was often used as a cinema. In one week in February, St. George's Hall was showing 'The Great British Army Official War Film. 'Advance of the Tanks and the Battle of the Ancre', A noble & wonderful record of the Great Autumn Battle and the Historic Introduction of the Tanks', with seats priced at 6d to 1s 6d.[15] The rival attraction at the Kozey Picture Palace was 'a thrilling 3 reel drama 'The Great Bank Robbery' followed by a 2 reel 'Bison Drama, At Mad Mule Canyon'.[16] At Christmas, St. George's Hall was used for Christmas 'kinematograph and variety entertainment' for the troops. 'On entering the door, each soldier or sailor was presented with a packet of cigarettes and an apple'.[17]

The Corporation, and others, were responsible for the formation of numerous allotment gardens, and many householders sacrificed their lawns and gardens for the cultivation of vegetables. However, much time and some bitterness was spent by the Corporation in a dispute with the County Education Committee, who refused to give the Corporation permission to requisition the High School's playing field for potato growing. The Mayor told the councillors that 'scores of people had been asking why this special piece of land at the Girls' High School was kept for certain particular young ladies to play hockey on' when it was only used about once a week and was ideal for growing potatoes. When it was suggested that a deputation should go to County Hall to argue the case, the Mayor said, 'If you want a deputation, don't put the Mayor on it, because I am not accustomed to ask as a favour what I should demand as a right. Go down on your knees to the County Council - not me!'[18] Mr. A.W. Chard was in his fifth year of office as Mayor, and it seems that the only reason why he was not elected for a sixth year was because his military duties took him away from the town. Over a year later, the argument over the playing field was rumbling on, with the Corporation grumbling at the County Education Committee's continuing refusal to hand it over for potato growing.[19]

In September 1917, considerable controversy was caused by the decision of the Lord Chancellor's office to merge the Falmouth and Truro County Courts. It was feared that sittings would no longer take place in Falmouth, and those who could ill afford the money or the time would have to travel to Truro to have their cases heard.[20] A letter from the Lord Chancellor's department laid these fears to rest - sittings would continue as before in Falmouth, but the administration would be done in Truro.

A Falmouth tradesman, with the splendidly Cornish name of Adolph Hans Jorgen Martins Sophus Petersen, was charged with an offence under Defence of the Realm regulations. It was alleged that in a conversation with a Mr. Hughes, Petersen maintained that Nurse Cavell had received her just deserts - 'she had been warned twice and a woman was worse than a man'. He went on to claim that the Germans only sank ships carrying contraband, and that they were entitled to do that. These remarks were deemed by the prosecution as 'likely to cause disaffection towards His Majesty'. Petersen was a Dane by birth, but was a naturalised British subject and had carried on an outfitter's business in Falmouth for many years, and had a son serving in the British Army in France. Petersen's defence was that the conversation with Hughes never took place, that he had been at home all the day in question and he produced several witnesses to testify that he was a loyal subject and, as a Dane by birth, had no reason to like the Germans. He did not know why Hughes should perjure himself, but that what was what he had done. The justices, having given 'anxious consideration to this case, could not help coming to the conclusion that Mr. Petersen does not possess the sentiments that anyone enjoying the protection of this country should possess, and they believe that Mr. Hughes's evidence is true. Disloyal statements of this kind cannot be allowed. Defendant will be fined £10'.[21]

The Russian Revolution in March 1917, and the abdication of the Tsar, did not weigh heavily with the editor of the *Packet* who gave these momentous events a small paragraph at the foot of the page, expressing the opinion that the Tsar's downfall was not due to the war itself, but rather that the Tsar 'had not prosecuted the War with the energy and efficiency expected by the people'.[22] Similarly, the entry of the USA into the war was mentioned only as part of a report of a service held at the Parish Church to mark 'America Day'.[23]

By April 1917, with the U-boat menace at its worst, and the necessity of increasing food production to ward off the spectre of starvation being recognised on all sides, up to five hundred soldiers, experienced ploughmen and the like, were temporarily released from military duties so that they could be employed on Cornish farms, to offset the loss of so many farm workers to the armed forces.[24] There was a national campaign during Easter Week 1917 to desist from eating eggs, and to donate them to the sick and wounded.[25] However, not everyone had their eye firmly on the war effort; there was a strike of the 60 employees of Falmouth & District Laundry, due to two colleagues being made redundant following the installation of labour saving equipment. This followed shortly after the employees had joined a union.[26] Two young ladies fell asleep in the sun on the rocks at Maenporth one afternoon, and when they awoke, they found that they were cut off by the incoming tide. Their cries for help were heard, and they were brought up the cliff face with ropes to safety.[27]

The Medical Officer of Health was much exercised by the high rate of infant mortality in the town. In 1915, infant death rate stood at 153 per 1000 births, and in 1916, 108, whilst the average for the country as a whole in 1916 was 91. In a town with the advantages of Falmouth, it was felt that this should be down to 50.[28] There was a big improvement in 1917, when the rate dropped to 60.3, which translated into 12 deaths of infants under one year. On the other hand, the number of births in Falmouth in 1917, 181, was the lowest on record,[29] which perhaps says a good deal for the moral standards of Falmouth women, with their menfolk away in the services, but with the town bursting with young soldiers and sailors. Penryn held a parade of babies in connection with the National Baby Week. The Mayor expressed the view that, as a result of the deaths of so many young men on the battle field, they must 'prize their boy babies especially, because they were the coming nation of Englishmen, and mothers should see to it that they were not allowed to grow up weaklings, but a virile race of men'. The county inspector of infant welfare, Miss Kennerly, spelt out the essentials for healthy babies - proper housing and sanitation, a larder in which to keep the food, and plenty of sunshine. Miss Day, the Falmouth health visitor, brought her audience down to earth with a stark statistic - 'all the year round a baby was dying every five minutes'.[30]

Another medical scourge was that of tuberculosis. There were 434 deaths from this disease in Cornwall in 1916, and it was said that there were two hundred or more former soldiers or sailors in the county who had been discharged from the services suffering from tuberculosis. When the fading fortunes of the Bassett family resulted in their mansion at Tehidy being put on the market, great efforts, ultimately successful, were made to purchase this for use as a sanatorium, and a grant of £50 was made from the Falmouth War Relief Committee towards this end.[31]

Canon H.H. King returned to the Parish Church after his long convalescence in the Canaries. He told of the privations of the Canary Islanders as a result of the war putting a stop to the fruit trade, 'thousands of people being in a state of semi-starvation... .One well known English firm, employing hundreds of men in the fruit trade, had gained great respect by keeping their work people on half pay, although no work was being done... . German propaganda in the islands was very strong and no stone was left unturned to throw odium on the Allies'. Nearly all the English doctors formerly working there were now either in France or Mesopotamia, and all young Englishmen had joined the forces. It took Canon King 15 days to make the journey home, travelling through France, as absolute priority was given on French trains to the military, and civilians are encouraged not to travel. Paris he found 'utterly changed', and was astonished to find girls acting as porters at French stations and handling 'the big cases like men'. Canon King claimed that he was kept under surveillance by French police, who were very suspicious of foreign civilians travelling in their country in time of war.[32] What might seem today to be a surprising slant on the war was provided by Canon King in his sermon at a service held to mark the third anniversary of the outbreak of war. He propounded the theory that 'the war has saved us... .I believe that we should say, thank God for this war'. In his view, the country in August 1914 was on the very brink of internal disaster:

'We were within an ace of falling upon our own flesh and blood: it is awful to think of. Men, who were brothers, were grasping their weapons and looking into the whites of each other's eyes, ready to slay. The air was electric. Ugly rumours were current about discipline in the Army. It was whispered that officers would not obey their orders under certain circumstances... .And then look at labour, a seething mass of discontent, strikes, riots and lock-outs following one another, until on the very eve of war a general railway strike throughout the country was proclaimed. Then one section of the community was embittered with another - one class set against another class, till the whole social frame was strained and quivering. Party political strife exceeded anything of the kind known before.

And what was it which suddenly - like a bolt from the blue - hushed every note of strife and made men hold their breath? It was war: war, which gave men other things to think of. War, which gave men other things to live for. War, which came like some beneficent surgeon's knife to cut out the unwholesome growth within the body politic, and drain it of the malignant blood that was poisoning its life. War! It was war which awoke the nation, and welded it together and gave it unity of direction, and will, and purpose. In war, the nation has found and proved itself'. The Church Militant indeed!

A Miss Carkeek addressed a meeting at Falmouth Wesley Church, claiming that 'there were too many easy chair Christians, that the Church had not risen to the occasion, and should it be said that it had failed in its duty and privilege in the hour of the nation's greatest need'? However, she believed that 'God was working out His great designs in the War... . The Union Jack floated over one fifth of the whole world and stood for unity, duty, freedom, self sacrifice and victory', but one of the greatest curses was the drink traffic. They wanted bread, yet in spite of that they were still brewing beer... if a man drank three quarts of beer, he drank another person's ration of grain and sugar'.[34]

It was a war in which both sides claimed the support of the Almighty. The poet, J.C. Squire, put the position very neatly in four lines:
'God heard the embattled nations sing and shout:
'Gott strafe England' - 'God save the King' -
'God this' - 'God that' - and 'God the other thing'.
'My God', said God, 'I've got my work cut out'.[35]

Among the many wartime restrictions, sketching was forbidden without a permit. John Badcock, a visitor from London, was unaware of this and there were no notices or posters to inform him of the restrictions. He therefore went out sketching a country scene and was promptly arrested and brought before the Falmouth magistrates, who clearly had every sympathy with him. One of the magistrates asked the Superintendent of Police how was Mr. Badcock to know that he was in breach of the regulations, to which the Superintendent replied, 'Everyone is supposed to know the law'. Forced to convict, the bench refused to impose a fine or any other penalty, and the Chairman told Mr. Badcock that he was very sorry that he had been a victim of circumstances.[36] However, a lady on a pleasure trip round the bay did not get off so lightly when she took photos of two warships. She was fined £10 and told that she ought to know better.[37]

Alderman J. Grose came in for withering criticism in the magazine *The Schoolmaster*. The Mayor had proposed 'certain small increases in the rate of remuneration of the Falmouth teachers', but Alderman Grose asked why they did not pay their teachers by the hour - 'other people in Falmouth worked for 8d an hour, whilst the teachers were getting about 4s an hour. If 8d per hour pays other people, it should pay them'. To which the teachers' magazine replied, 'We are not aware what profession or vocation is honoured by the services of Mr. J. Grose, or how much per hour is regarded by him as suitable remuneration for his services. But he is probably not a member of any more necessary or honourable profession than that of teaching, and we suggest that if he is at the present moment remunerated at the rate of more than 8d per hour, he should show earnest in his remarks by relinquishing the surplus. Falmouth is a delightful place, exceedingly old fashioned, and a Captain Marryat kind of port. It used to be famous for its curiosities, among which, we imagine, Mr. Grose might well be counted now'.[38]

The tourist industry continued to benefit from the fact that Cornwall was far removed from the threat posed by Zeppelins and raids by warships, as many who would have gone to the east and south coast resors were now coming to the far west. However, in August 1917 Falmouth and the other Cornish resorts were enjoying only 'a fairly successful season' because of the very wet summer.[39]

Commander Norman Craig MP gave an address at a garden party held at Gyllyngdune in aid of the War Hospital Supply Depot. He concentrated on the iniquities of Germany - 'She had broken all laws, human and divine. Military necessity had been her only rule. Deliberate frightfulness, awfulness and cruelty had been practised, and people had been driven, down trodden, before the Kaiser's chariot. She had put down hospital and passenger ships and even struck a medal to celebrate their shame. Wells had been poisoned, and the crowning shame of all was the dropping from air machines of poisoned sweets so that babies could pick them up and disseminate disease and death'.[40]

As food became scarcer, bitter controversy arose regarding alleged 'profiteering' by farmers. The price of milk, 6d a quart, was described in a letter to the *Packet* as 'exhorbitant and uncalled for... Farmers who honestly speak out will tell you that they have never known such prosperity... Whilst our fighting men are feverishly endeavouring to win through to victory, many at home are as feverishly anxious to get rich'.[41] A Mr. Mellow wrote to the *Briton* defending the farmer. 'Before prices were fixed, he sold his cattle in the open market. He had nothing whatever to do with fixing the price; the law of supply and demand did that. Is this profiteering? What is his position today? Now that the price is fixed for what he has to sell, and no attempt has been made to fix the price for what he has to buy, the inevitable will surely happen and, if the cost of production is greater than the fixed price, say of £3 per live hundredweight for fat cattle, then the cattle will not be fed'. His complaint that 'the majority of people in this country worshipped at the shrine of cheapness, and did not care what became of agriculture' resonates today.[42]

It was in 1917 that wartime austerity began to bite seriously, with shortages of sugar, potatoes, margarine and coal, 'serious enough to bring a new phenomenon upon the civic scene, the queue'. Schemes of voluntary or local authority rationing were introduced, but these proved insufficient and in April 1918 a compulsory rationing system came in, with the weekly meat ration fixed at three-quarters of a pound. 'All through the war recipes for such revolutionary delicacies as haricot bean fritters, savoury oatmeal pudding and barley rissoles were much publicised'. Bread, after December 1916, was 'Government Bread', which contained such ingredients as potato flour or bean flour, which soon deteriorated in warm weather. Margarine largely replaced butter, and there was even Government Control Tea. There was at no time widespread privation, and the effect of shortages and rationing was to spread standards of nutrition as between social classes.

Where wartime restrictions had a much deeper and more enduring effect was in their impingement upon the sale of alcoholic liquor. Before the war, public houses in Falmouth were open from 6.00am until 11.00pm. However, once the war began it was realised that alcohol was having a huge effect on industrial, and particularly munition, production, and also on the training of the new armies in this country. As Lloyd George put it in March 1915, the country was faced by three foes, Germany, Austria and Drink, and the deadliest was Drink. 'Men come late or absent themselves for days, and drink is the lure that has drawn them from their duties... Through one man being off on a drinking bout, seventy men were forced to be idle'.[43] It was claimed that the nation spent eight million pounds more on drink in the first half of 1915, than it had done in the corresponding period in 1914.[44] There was pressure to bring in total prohibition on the grounds that, if licensing hours were simply reduced, men would 'crowd their drinking into shorter hours', and that it was owed to the men at the front who 'have a right to expect that we at home will put country before every consideration, and know how to make sacrifices'.[45] However, by Acts of Parliament in 1914 and 1915, regulations were brought in limiting the sale of alcohol to two and a half hours in the middle of the day and to three hours in the evening, restrictions which were made permanent by the Licensing Act, 1921. Special restrictions were placed upon spirits, including a maximum potency of 70 degrees proof, and a prohibition on sales at weekends. A pint of beer cost 3 pence in July 1914; by 1917, a pint, drastically reduced in gravity and known derisively as 'Government Ale', cost 7 pence. The price of spirits, during the war, multiplied four or five times. However, the 'closing' times varied from place to place, with pubs closing in Falmouth at 9.00pm and in Truro at 11.00pm in February 1916. It seems that when the pubs closed in Falmouth, parties would drive to Truro and 'gathered together in a semi-intoxicated state and were a nuisance to the neighbourhood', according to the Chief Constable, who then complained of 'people kissing and embracing in the street' after 11.00pm which he considered prejudicial to public moral welfare. He persuaded the Truro licensing justices to fall into line with Falmouth and to order closing at 9.00pm.[46] In May 1916 'summer time' was introduced, giving longer and lighter evenings, and this too became a permanent institution.

The unions did not miss the opportunity handed to them by the war, when their active cooperation was vital for the very survival of the country, to use their bargaining power to increase wages, so that in industry wage rates at the end of the war had roughly doubled, keeping just ahead of rising prices. 'Sales among the working classes of pianos - that coveted proof of respectability - fur coats, gramophones and motor-bicycles boomed'. However, this relative prosperity did not relate to those families for which the principal wage earner was in the armed forces, as their pay did not keep up with prices. From the autumn of 1915, women began to earn good money in occupations opened to them by the departure of men to the front. There was a boom in cinema going, which before the war had been, essentially, 'the poor man's theatre', but in the war years became equally a middle class entertainment, and the new purchasing power of women, and their relative independence, also vastly increased cinema audiences. An increase in gambling came from increased incomes and from a reduction in the consumption of alcohol. Whilst the war lasted, the churches were crowded, but the pre-war decline in church attendance accelerated thereafter, principally as a reaction against the blatant war time jingoism of the churches.[47]

The government had been very reluctant to bring in food rationing, and its focus had been on guns and munitions, with the result, as the *Briton* put it, that the government had been busy with 'feeding the guns' and had overlooked feeding the people. The grain shortage had caught the government on the hop, and appeals to eat less bread did not have the success envisaged; in fact the average weekly consumption had gone up from 5 lbs 6oz per person before the war to 6lbs per person in April 1917. The reason for this was that the poorest in the community could not afford the prices of the substitutes for bread urged by the government, beans, rice, pulses etc, which in some cases had increased by 400%, and so fell back on the cheapest food they knew, bread. The government had also failed to encourage a massive increase in home grown foodstuffs, and although the price of potatoes was controlled, in many parts of the country they simply could not be bought. 'It is hardly too much to say that the Government's interference with the food problem so far has been a gigantic muddle. There has been no reduction in the consumption of wheat and other cereals, while the prices of food generally have gone flying to unheard of heights'.[48] The government policy of exhorting people to eat less bread without backing it up with rationing was bitterly criticised by the *Briton* 'And so the wait and see goes on while the stocks of wheat grow less and the destruction of our vessels by German submarines continues. When the Cabinet awoke to the position a few months ago there ought to have been far more drastic measures enforced than have ever yet been taken'.[49]

The *Briton* also warned against extravagant hopes for the future, after the war. 'Often we read speeches of what is going to happen after the war. The effusions are the outcome of sanguine temperaments and a total disregard of the lessons of history. After the war there will be a period of trade depression, not only in England, but in every European country engaged in the war. They have spent their resources at a lavish rate during the past two years, and when the war is over will be faced by debts and devastated countries. It is better to recognise this fact now and prepare to meet the situation when it arises, than to be misled by perfervid orators whose predictions are the outcome of fancy'.[50]

Mrs. B.L. Gregor, the wife of the Medical Officer of Health, brought a hornet's nest about her ears by criticising the culinary habits of working class women, and by suggesting that they wasted food, as was proved, in her view, by an examination of their dustbins. This brought a spate of letters to the *Packet* from such as 'A Working Man's Wife', 'One of the Workers' and 'One Who Is Willing to Learn'. One wrote, 'We are four in family; the eldest is an apprentice in a foundry and has his breakfast at six o clock in the morning before he goes to work and takes his midday meal with him, coming home at six in the evening. The other two children go to school. Will Mrs. Gregor tell me how she would manage in my case on 24s a week, and give the menu daily?' Mrs. Gregor's suggestion of a 'nourishing meal of soup' at midday was ridiculed by the wife of a man who had to work all the afternoon digging potatoes or carrying coal'. Another maintained that 'we do not exist entirely on pasties... and where can one pennyworth of cheese be bought... Our potato peelings and turnip skins go to save the coal, which is, like most things, dear... Our husbands in the home or in the fighting line are better and finer men on a full stomach than on an empty one.' Another wrote that Mrs. Gregor and her class 'haven't the faintest idea of what a working man's home really is' and that it would make a working man cry at his wife's extravagance if he came 'to dinner to find, ready for his consumption, one pennyworth of cheese, two pennyworth of barley, two pennyworth of bones and an onion'. Another defended the Cornish pasty, which Mrs. Gregor had condemned as wasteful 'we hesitate to believe that much of its good properties can be lost when it is properly cooked' and went on, 'To be a member of the working class does not imply, necessarily, ignorance of food values. We cannot live on soup, even if we could always obtain the material for making it'.[51]

Mrs. Gregor stuck to her guns in a long reply printed in the *Packet*, claiming that her critics had deliberately misunderstood what she had originally written, and that her suggestions applied to everyone - 'rich and poor are alike in wartime stress - for what avail is money with little or no food to buy?' In her view, Falmouth had not felt 'the real pinch of war', things being much worse in the big cities where 'the despised knuckle or shin bone, boiled with barley is already a luxury'. Mrs. Gregor went on to say that 'I have no wish to hurt or belittle the working man's wife, all honour to her efforts, but long years of cheap food have made her careless of food values and so there is bound to be waste... It is a question of buying the right kind of food and cooking it in the best possible way. It is this right way which makes all the difference. It is what the middle classes study and the working classes as a rule do not'.[52] However, this public controversy forced Mrs. Gregor to resign from the Falmouth Food Control Committee, stating in her letter to the executive officer, 'Since all that correspondence in the papers, I find that all I do, or say, is received with opprobrium and resentment by the working classes. Rude remarks are thrown at me in the streets, and vulgar anonymous letters are sent me by post. Without reason they are convinced that I am out to 'pinch the poor' and feed the rich'. In accepting her resignation, whilst stating that such insults were entirely undeserved, the committee did comment that 'Mrs. Gregor's facts and figures might not have been put exactly as clearly as some of them (the members) might be able to put them and, in her eagerness to prove her case, possibly she overstated rather than understated them'.[53]

Mrs. Gregor was a formidable lady, as a burglar found when he climbed in at her bedroom window in Melville Road at 1.30am. Confronted by Mrs. Gregor, he fled but was soon apprehended by the police and within the hour brought back to the house to apologise to Mrs. Gregor, who 'told him to be a Briton not a thief'.[54]

NOTES

[1] FP, 29.12.1916, p3
[2] FP, 2.4.1917
[3] FP, 2.2.1917
[4] FP, 21.12.1917, p3
[5] FP, 19.1.1917, p2
[6] WB, 25.6.1917, p2
[7] WB, 22.3.1917
[8] WB, 8.1.1917, p3
[9] WB, 19.4.1917, p6
[10] FP, 6.4.1917, p4
[11] WB, 11.6.1917, p1
[12] WB, 3.5.1917, p5
[13] WB, 18.2.1917, p5
[14] FP, 16.2.1917, p2
[15] FP, 23.2.1917, p2
[16] FP, 23.2.1917, p1
[17] FP, 28.12.1917, p3
[18] FP, 16.2.1917, p3
[19] FP, 17.5.1918, p3
[20] FP, 28.9.1917, p3
[21] FP, 2.3.1917, p3
[22] FP, 16.3.1917, p3
[23] FP, 27.4.1917, p3
[24] WB, 5.4.1917, p4
[25] WB, 5.4.1917, p4
[26] WB, 26.4.1917, p5
[27] WB, 26.4.1917, p5
[28] FP, 11.5.1917, p4

[29] FP, 17.5.1918, p4
[30] FP, 13.7.1917, p3
[31] FP, 21.12.1917, p3
[32] FP, 1.6.1917, p4
[33] FP, 10.8.1917, p3
[34] FP, 26.10.1917, p4
[35] J.C. Squire, quoted by A.J.P. Taylor, The First World War, p65
[36] WB, 2.7.1917, p1
[37] WB, 10.9.1917, p3
[38] FP, 3.8.1917, p2
[39] WB, 13.8.1917, p2
[40] FP, 21.9.1917, p3
[41] FP, 2.11.1917, p3
[42] FP, 19.10.1917, p4
[43] WB, 3.4.1915, p2
[44] WB, 14.2.1916, p2
[45] WB, 14.2.1916, p2
[46] WB, 10.2.1916, p3
[47] Arthur Marwick, 'British Life & Leisure in the First World War', History Today, June 1965, pp409-419
[48] WB, 30.4.1917, p2
[49] WB, 30.4.1917, p2
[50] WB, 30.4.1917, p2
[51] FP, 16.11.1917, p3
[52] FP, 23.11.1917, p3
[53] FP, 21.12.1917, p4
[54] WB, 30.12.1915, p6

CHAPTER XIII

RATIONING

On the eve of war, in 1914, Britain imported two thirds of its food, measured in calories.[1] Whilst the general public were exhorted in war time to eat less and grow more, the country still depended for very life itself on merchant shipping bringing in essential food and materials, and by early 1917 the huge losses of such shipping to U-boat attacks brought the spectre of starvation. Enormous quantities of meat, grain and sugar were sent to the sea bottom, and the country had food stocks to last only a few weeks. The government made every effort to avoid compulsory rationing of food, arguing that prices and distribution could be kept under control 'if food economy is exercised in every household'. In May 1917, a letter was sent to every household from the Ministry of Food appealing for economy in the consumption of bread - 'The enemy is trying to take away our daily bread. He is sinking our wheat ships. If he succeeds in starving us, our soldiers will have died in vain'.[2] The authorities first resorted to detailed regulations fixing the prices at which commodities could be sold, which resulted in prosecutions for selling margarine without a licence, for selling milk at above the maximum price laid down (4½d a quart in June 1918),[3] similarly beer (4d or 5d a pint in July 1918, depending on its strength) and cigarettes (20 Players, maximum price 10½d.).[4] But this price fixing required a mushrooming bureaucracy - 'think what has happened over sugar. Grocers and their customers have been almost distracted by orders, cards, and forms. And armies of clerks and officials have been spending months on collection, tabulation and explanation. Life would be next to unbearable if the same amount of confusion and work was created by each of the many food articles we require'.[5]

These maximum prices did not always work to the advantage of the ordinary Falmouthian. The *West Briton* made the point that Cornwall produced many items of food which, before the imposition of maximum prices, sold for less, but as soon as price regulation came in, the price of these items went up to the maximum permitted.[6] Another problem arose when those prices were fixed at so low a level that it was not worth the wholesalers or the retailers stocking the items concerned. Thus, there were widespread shortages of cheese, margarine and canned beef - as the *Briton* put it, 'we want food at a reasonably low price; but low price without the food will not satisfy hunger'.[7] The sale of cream was banned between December 1917 and April 1918 in order to conserve stocks of whole milk.[8] Whilst the making and sale of ice cream was permitted throughout the summer of 1917, it was banned in December when few wanted it; as the *Briton* said, 'It is worthy of a comic opera. We have all laughed heartily at things not half as ridiculous on the stage'.[9] Taxis were permitted only to travel 3 miles from the town.[10] The throwing of rice at weddings was forbidden, and prosecutions brought to enforce this.[11] Restaurants were forbidden to serve meat dishes on specified days, although this order was rescinded in May 1918 when meat rationing for all came in.[12] One of the more bizarre campaigns was for the saving and collection of nut shells and fruit stones. It seems that these could be converted into charcoal which could then be used in the manufacture of gas masks. 'The charcoal thus produced greatly increases our soldiers' chances of coming through gas attacks'.[13]

Fortunately, almost in the nick of time, the introduction of the convoy system in May 1917 drastically reduced the losses in merchant shipping, and by the autumn the immediate threat of starvation was lifted. In July 1917 a new rationing scheme was forwarded to the Local Food Control Committees for adoption. The principal features were: (1) That every customer should be registered with one shop for the purchase of each item of food stuff and not be allowed to buy it elsewhere; (2) The shopkeeper was to divide his weekly supplies in proportion among all customers registered with him; (3) No shopkeeper to be allowed to register more customers than he could conveniently serve. At various times prices were regulated for most food stuffs. Tradesmen and public were undoubtedly much harassed and strained by the various irksome restrictions and regulations. Food hoarding became an offence; anyone with a supply of any of the staple articles for more than three weeks was deemed to be hoarding and subject to prosecution, and specially appointed food inspectors, together with the police, had the power to inspect the larders of any who they thought might be hoarding food. Prosecutions also occurred for selling articles above the price fixed as a maximum. Falmouth being a 'prescribed area' subject to liquor control, intoxicating liquor could only be sold on weekdays between 12.00 noon and 2.30pm and between 6.00pm and 8.00pm, and on Sundays between 12.30pm and 2.30 pm, and a customer at his local could no longer put drinks 'on the slate' - no credit was allowed. Towards the end of 1917, the maximum retail price of coal was fixed, and in July 1918 gas and electricity were rationed upon the basis of coal consumption. There was an enormous demand for waste paper, which was required, among other things, for munitions, and the Corporation and local library were urged to release for repulping all used papers, books etc., which it was no longer necessary to retain.[14]

The food shortages of the war caused the birth of the lasting affection of the British for the queue. Long queues for margarine outside Lipton's caused controversy. 'One old man was pushing and shouldering in a way that was unbecoming and unnecessary', according to the Executive Officer of the Falmouth Food Control Committee who 'thought it was time to take action and commandeered 3cwt of margarine and distributed it to various shops. He then told the people to go to those shops, but not one person moved and he was persuaded by the way the people carried on that they liked being in the crowd, for they joked and laughed for all they were worth'.[15] The sequel to this was a claim by Lipton's against the Food Control Committee for an extra 1d for each pound of margarine seized by the Executive Officer, but liability was repudiated by the Committee.[16] The question whether wrapping paper for a loaf of bread could be charged for under wartime regulations remained unanswered by the magistrates, when a baker was accused of charging (properly) 4½d for a loaf, and a further ½d for the wrapping. The case was dismissed and the police were asked to look into the matter.[17]

Whilst food prices were regulated, food rationing came in very late in the war, in February 1918, and then only on a piecemeal basis. In the same month, representatives of Food Control Committees in West Cornwall, including Falmouth and Penryn, met and passed a resolution 'that the time had arrived for the adoption of a local scheme of rationing, that such scheme should be uniform, that committees be recommended to adopt the London scheme, and that a joint advisory committee be set up to consider the question of supplies'.[18]

The winter of 1917-18 was very cold with plenty of snow, and the inclement weather added to the bitter complaints over the quality of coal delivered to Cornwall. At a meeting to discuss the economic use of coal, it was pointed out that it was impossible to make economies when the fuel was 'absolute rubbish and quite unburnable', being small coal and slate in about equal proportions and sold at best house coal prices. It was alleged that the Welsh colliery owners sent to Cornwall supplies taken from the heaps of waste thrown aside at the pit head as useless, and it was agreed to ask the Coal Controller 'to see that we are not again victimised by the collieries'.[19] The threat of drastic coal shortages during the winter of 1918-19 brought forth considerable criticism both of the miners, or colliers as they were then known, and of the government. The official line that the shortages were due to so many colliers then being in the Army was not believed, and the complaint grew strength that there were more than enough colliers left in the industry, many of whom it was alleged worked only three days a week, to produce all the coal the nation needed. The reaction of the government to the impending crisis was not to get more work out of the existing work force but to draft colliers back from the Army to the coalfields. 'These men have been trained (as soldiers) at enormous cost to the nation. Now colliers are to be drawn from the Army at the rate of 2,000 a day to work in the mines. And that is how we get on with the war!'[20] By the beginning of April 1919, the coal situation had become desperate in Falmouth, due to a coal carrying steamer, *Falmouth Castle*, running aground, and there was only one week's supply left. Fresh supplies were brought in by sea and rail to meet the crisis, but there was no option but to pay substantially over the controlled price for this.[21]

As the visitors flooded into Falmouth in summer 1918, it was not always easy to feed them, because although they brought their ration coupons with them, some of the food stuffs were in short supply.[22] Further difficulties were caused by the complete failure of the apple and plum crops, although it was a bumper year for blackberries.[23] The Food Controller decreed a flat rate across the country for milk of 2s 6d per gallon to the consumer, which was far higher than was being paid in Cornwall. 'This is beyond everything that was expected and should not be meekly endured'.[24] However the milk producers were far from satisfied, and in May 1919 there was an attempt on the part of the producers to withhold their milk, and 'Falmouth rose in its wrath against the dealers'. The Executive Officer of the Food Committee requisitioned supplies of milk, and advised customers to switch to those producers who were still prepared to supply their customers, although one of these was threatened with having his milk float turned over when he tried to bring supplies into the town. The dispute did not last long, but not before the dealers' actions were described at a public meeting as 'a Hunnish act... . Public opinion broke the back of the strike on Monday and on Tuesday most of the dairymen returned to their rounds, only to find, however, that many people had transferred their custom to the loyal dealers who met their needs on the previous day'.[25] The ration of butter was 1oz. per person per week, jam was rationed and potato flour was added to wheat flour to make bread.

The difficulties in obtaining certain foods, and more particularly the intricacies of wartime restrictions weighed heavily on the civilian population. This anxiety and exasperation can be judged from the fact that the local newspapers, week after week, were obsessed with food in all its forms. A man returning from the front on leave could be forgiven for thinking that food, or the difficulties appertaining to it, dominated the public consciousness more that the tremendous and bloody battles being fought across the Channel. Perhaps it was easier to express grumbles and exasperation over petty regulations, than the ceaseless anxiety and anguish for husbands, fathers and brothers at the front or on the high seas.

The widespread impression that farmers were not doing enough to feed the nation was belied by official figures released by the Board of Agriculture shortly after the Armistice. These showed that in 1918 there was an increase of more than 1,700,000 acres under corn compared with 1914, and that the acreage producing potatoes had gone up from 462,000 in 1914 to 634,000 in 1918. In addition, the number of cattle had increased during the same period by half a million, although the number of sheep had slightly decreased, and there were approaching one million less pigs.[26] Rationing eventually came to an end on 30th June 1919.[27]

NOTES

1 Richard Van Emden & Steve Humphries, *All Quiet On The Home Front*, p189
2 Ministry of Food Circular No. 67, dated 29th May 1917
3 FP, 7.6.1918, p2
4 FP, 26.7.1918, p4
5 WB, 17.12.1917, p2
6 WB, 19.11.1917, p2
7 WB, 18.2.1918, p2
8 WB, 26.11.1917, p3
9 WB, 7.1.1918, p2
10 FP, 28.6.1918, p2
11 WB, 11.4.1918, p5
12 WB, 23.5.1918, p7
13 WB, 15.8.1918, p6
14 Wilson Lloyd Fox, 'Falmouth and the Great War', undated
15 FP, 29.3.1918, p4
16 WB, 21.11.1918, p4
17 FP, 31.5.1918, p2
18 FP, 15.2.1918, p4
19 WB, 27.5.1918, p2
20 WB, 16.9.1918, p2
21 WB, 3.4.1919, p3
22 WB, 19.8.1918, p2
23 WB, 2.9.1918, p2
24 WB, 23.9.1918, p2
25 WB, 15.5.1919, p4
26 WB, 2.11.1919, p2
27 WB, 17.4.1919, p7

CHAPTER XIV

PLANS OR DREAMS?
THE DEVELOPMENT OF THE PORT

In May 1914, the architect of the modern British Navy, Admiral Lord Fisher, wrote a lengthy appraisal of policy for the Admiralty, in which he foresaw the difficulties and dangers which the life line of merchant shipping in time of war would run, if they had to proceed up the Channel before discharging their cargoes. Fisher wrote,

'It is very desirable that full consideration should be promptly given to the question of diverting our commerce to our far western ports in wartime, and of developing the port and railway facilities of such harbours as Falmouth... . This precaution alone would ensure that the hostile submarine - if German - must commence to operate at a distance of nearly 1,000 miles from his base, and although a submarine can do so, yet it remains quite true that it is a very serious disability'.[1]

It seems extraordinary now, with the benefit of hindsight, that Churchill, as First Lord of the Admiralty, dismissed Fisher's thesis because he did not believe that submarines would ever be used by a civilised power to sink merchant ships. Churchill described this as 'an unthinkable proposition' and wrote to Fisher, 'the excellence of your paper is, to some extent, marred by the prominence assigned to it'.[2]

In March 1916, the Chamber of Commerce debated how the port of Falmouth could benefit in the long term from development. The war had shown that the harbour was capable of much greater use, accommodating 'some of the biggest liners afloat... Two United States battleships and 40 or 50 big cargo steamers had had berths found for them about the same time... the time was never more opportune than now to be up and doing'.[3] It was felt that the relatively close proximity of the great naval base of Plymouth ruled out any possibility of Falmouth being developed by the Navy. Also, the lack of coal and industry in the area was a drawback, but one that did not prevent the development of large scale ship building facilities, or the construction of manufacturing industries, the raw materials for which could easily be brought in by sea. It was appreciated that Falmouth was less happily placed than London, Bristol, Southampton, Liverpool, Hull and the Tyne for goods to be transported to and from the port by rail, so 'the new docks would have to rely upon the coastwise distribution and collection of goods carried overseas to and from the docks by the great ocean steamships... This systematised cooperation on a large scale of the ocean and coasting trades is merely a development of what is already being done from the ports now used by the ocean liners'. It was argued that if adequate facilities were provided, the changes in trade brought on by the war would result in far greater use of Falmouth as a major shipping centre, and in particular that the docks could be used as the central home port for Canadian and other colonial produce.

The debate continued at the Chamber's AGM in April. The chairman, Mr. J.H. Lake, stated that he did not believe that the prosperity of the town had suffered because it was a long way from the commercial centres - 'it was because the Falmouth Harbour Board of forty years ago had betrayed their trust towards the town. When Falmouth was a flourishing port, Liverpool was a fishing village, and, while they had been thinking, Liverpool had forged ahead without quibbling or quarrelling. Whilst Falmouth had been silting up, Padstow had gone ahead'. The future of the merchant navy lay with big 30,000 ton ships to carry the grain from American ports, and interested parties were already looking at Falmouth, to see if the port could accommodate these giants. This would require some dredging work, but this would be relatively cheap compared with the ensuing benefits. These great ships must have a deep water port, 'and Falmouth harbour was within 400 yards of the deepest water in the world'. Mr. Lake said that they must now look ahead 'and see if they could not get Falmouth made a great naval port, coaling station and a place for exports'. Mr. C. Spargo did not agree with the chairman. In his view, the harbour could not be put to its proper use unless it was adjacent to a big manufacturing centre, and it was precisely because Liverpool and Bristol were so adjacent that they had flourished, and Falmouth had not. It was no use hoping that after the war the present liner trade would continue; they were only calling at Falmouth at the present time because Southampton was closed to them. 'The only thing that he thought they could do was to induce the Government to make their port a naval one - (hear, hear). From a common sense point of view he did not see how it was possible for Falmouth to become a great mercantile port and a great business centre for the export of goods'. The secretary, Mr. F.J. Bowles, drew attention to the development of the town both as a holiday and a residential resort - 'Today people came to Falmouth not only because they wanted to live as long as possible, but also they found the place had most pleasant surroundings. Any scheme for the future prosperity of Falmouth would not be complete if it did not deal with the development of the place as a residential centre, not only for the wealthy, but for those possessed of moderate means... The commercial men of Falmouth must always remember that the town had a certain asset in the development of their scenery and surroundings'.

Mr. Julyan Polglase, in a letter to the *Packet* in May 1916, argued that if the docks had been fully developed by 1915, the *Lusitania* would not have had to enter the U-boat infested waters of the Irish Sea, but could have made for Falmouth, with the result that 'that vessel would now have been afloat instead of at the bottom of the ocean with many another good ship sunk by the enemy'. Mr. Polglase had earlier pointed out in a pamphlet on the development of Falmouth as a major port:

'In the event of war with a continental power, the possession of deep water commercial docks at the entrance of the English Channel, to which our foodstuffs and other necessaries can be brought in comparative safety and where our great cargo vessels, transports and passenger liners can be safely docked, will be of immense importance to the nation'.[4]

The *Packet* had given up 'leaders' in 1915, because of lack of space due to print restrictions, except for occasional subjects which the editor deemed of special importance. One such occasion was the question of food supply, and the huge losses caused by German submarines, threatening the ability of the country to continue the war, and in particular the losses suffered when a ship had arrived safely at an English port, but then had left for another port of discharge and was sunk on this second journey. Many of these unlucky ships had arrived safely at Falmouth in the first place, and it clearly made sense for them to discharge their cargoes there, instead of risking a second voyage. The *Packet* acknowledged that the present facilities for discharging cargoes was limited, as was the single track railway line to Truro, but 'what is there to prevent the Government from running out suitable wharves, providing dock accommodation and up to date appliances, doubling the line to Truro and furnishing the necessary manual labour from the numerous labour battalions?... If the Government could be persuaded to recognise the natural advantages of Falmouth over other Channel ports the necessary facilities could be provided in a very short period'.[5]

A local man, George Stock, then produced a pamphlet, 'The Necessity of a Strategical Port: Falmouth the Port'. Stock began by setting out the German submarine menace, which he foresaw as shifting the balance of power 'from Whitehall to Wilhelmstrasse'. As a result, Britain either had to produce all she needed herself, an impossibility, or certain ports had to be kept open and safe for the discharge of all imported goods. No port was better situated for this than Falmouth, 'being the largest and the finest natural harbour in the United Kingdom, and being such that it is the first port of call for all ships coming from America through the western 'sea lane' or from Australia, New Zealand and the Cape through the southern 'sea lane'... and Falmouth is at the junction of these sea lanes'. 'The Government should see that steps are taken immediately that the Port of Falmouth be developed, not so much from the point of view as a commercial port, but as part of the entire scheme of naval strategy as a means of keeping an open and safe port for the import of raw materials and foodstuffs into Great Britain during this war or any future war, which strategy has been brought about entirely through the partial transfer of power from the surface water man-of-war to the undersea submarine. A vital first step would be the construction of new railway lines from all the main centres to Falmouth'. Stock appreciated that if ship building, especially in America, did not outstrip losses due to U-boat warfare, the outlook was dire, but his longer term solution was novel - the large scale construction of submarine merchantmen each capable of carrying two or three thousand tons of goods. In the short term, and in the longer term, 'it seems as though nature has endowed this favoured port with a harbour and natural facilities of strategical value, which, with developments, such as mechanical contrivances, elevators, and the building of quays and docks, affords an ideal sheltered harbour over an enormous area'.[6]

The *Western Morning News*, in a review of 1917 in Falmouth, drew attention to 'the general criticism of the practice of allowing vessels laden with foodstuffs to call at home ports and then proceed to other destinations with possible risk of total loss by enemy craft', and stated that an investigation into the development of docking and rail facilities at Falmouth by a government commissioner had taken place, but no decision had yet been made. 'The submarine warfare had been brought home to Falmouthians more vividly than to most people in the country, because of the number of crews of wrecked and damaged vessels landed and cared for there, and also because of the presence in the harbour of ships which had been damaged, but fortunately not sunk by the enemy'.[7]

Great changes took place at the Falmouth Docks Company in early 1918. The chairman for the last 40 years, Mr. Howard Fox, and the long serving secretary, Mr. F.J. Bowles, both retired, and the company was taken over by a powerful shipping combine, the Federal Shipping Company, headed by Lord Inchcape. The Dock Company had had a chequered career; it had been incorporated in 1859, and carried out extensive improvements and additions, but, as a result of heavy damage in storms, the directors were obliged to inform the Board of Trade in December 1867 that 'the whole structure was in danger and that they had no prospect of raising funds for repairs'. The Board then took full possession and managed the docks, through a local committee, until the last day of 1915, when the Board's loan having been repaid in full, the docks were handed back to the Company. Two years later Lord Inchcape's concern took over the company, and although there may be dispute as to whether or not the assets were acquired at a sixth of their real value, as alleged by Mr. Howard Fox, the fact remains that in the nearly sixty years of the Company's existence, the long suffering shareholders had never received a single dividend on their investment.[8]

This take-over engendered huge optimism for the future of Falmouth as a port. The Corporation passed a resolution to the effect that it had heard 'with pleasure' of the take-over 'and pledges itself to cooperate with the Company in every way in its power for the extension and promotion of the trade of the port'. The members thought that the Company had passed into the hands of people with the money and expertise to develop fully the great natural harbour and to bring great prosperity to the town. Councillor Rickard said that 'Falmouth should prepare itself to burst its sides to make arrangements for the extensions that were to come', and the Town Clerk claimed that the take-over made Falmouth the most important town in the county, 'and they all hoped that they would become the most important town in the south west'. Getting further carried away, Councillor Belletti declared that Falmouth 'was coming into its own and that it would be *the* port of the United Kingdom'.9

Even the *Briton* asserted that 'there is practically no limit to the position that Falmouth may attain when once its geographical importance in the world's economy has been realised by the proper authorities', going on to make the point that, apart from the Falmouth packet service, virtually no use had been made over the centuries of one of the world's finest harbours.10 The Admiralty had taken over the docks for the duration of the war, for which they paid compensation of a lump sum of £400 plus annual sums of £3,600,11 and it was confidently expected that the experience of the war would oblige the Admiralty to develop Falmouth as a permanent naval base.12 It was in fact the Admiralty who made the first offer to purchase the docks, but then stood aside when a big commercial company expressed a keen interest, and this was greeted with pleasure by local businessmen, as it was thought that the Admiralty would have no interest in developing the commercial possibilities. The decision to sell the docks to Lord Inchcape's company was seen, with the utmost confidence, as the securing of the major development of Falmouth as a port. 'The purchase of the docks by shipping men of world wide fame will cause the growth to be comparatively rapid, and we may count upon Falmouth attaining to something like the importance in shipping affairs which its situation warrants'.13 The possibility of Falmouth taking over from Plymouth as the leading south western port was confidently predicted, and the former shareholders were praised for their 'far sighted and patriotic policy' in selling for far less than the assets of the company were worth, in order to open the door to major development.14

The great use of Falmouth by both mercantile and naval shipping in the war years, together with the take-over of the docks company by such a prestigious concern as that of Lord Inchcape had created an air of confidence that 'at last the port is likely to regain some of the glory it enjoyed in days of long ago'. In addition, a vast scheme for the development of the St. Just side of the harbour, involving the construction of a railway to connect up with the Great Western main line near Grampound Road and to serve the proposed new wharves and warehouses, was the subject of a parliamentary bill. This idea was not a new one; a bill along the same lines had been passed by the parliamentary officials for first reading in early 1914, but the war had seen to it that no further progress could be made.15 In May 1919, the St. Just (Falmouth) Ocean Wharves and Railway Bill was approved by a Select Committee of the House of Lords. The object of the Bill was to construct 3,800 feet of deep water wharves at St. Just, with subsidiary works, and to connect the wharves with the Great Western by constructing a railway 21 miles in length. Counsel for the promoters of the Bill stated that these wharves were intended to accommodate the largest ships engaged in commerce at all states of the tide, and would also provide an outlet for the china clay industry, to replace the existing rather inefficient one at Fowey, where clay had to be put into small ships and then transhipped at a deep water port for America and elsewhere. The importance of the china clay industry to the scheme could hardly be overestimated, as by 1913, over 900,000 tons were being exported annually, and this was expected to increase rapidly in the post-war years. This vast export trade was expected to be matched by the import through the new port of the huge amounts of coal required by the industry.

The estimated cost of the construction of the wharves and the railway was £1,500,000, and it was planned to start construction within five years and complete the scheme within ten. The scheme was supported by the County Council, most of the local authorities and by trade unions, but was opposed by the GWR and the Falmouth Docks Company. The attitude of the GWR seems rather dog in a manger, as that company would not provide the new line itself and objected to anyone else doing so, but the Falmouth Docks Company feared that such a huge development would transform the existing docks into a backwater.[16] The *Briton*, having agreed with the majority view that the scheme would be of great benefit not only to the china clay trade but would also provide a liner terminal, then went on to extol the advantages which the new railway line would bring to agriculture and general trade in the district, with intermediate stations planned at Philleigh, Tregony and Grampound, and 'a charming neighbourhood including St. Mawes, Gerrans, Veryan and Portscatho will be within easy reach of those who year after year make Cornwall their holiday resort'. In opposition to the view of the Falmouth Docks Company in objecting to the St. Just scheme, it was argued that the development of the existing docks and the St. Just scheme were complimentary. St. Just would accommodate ships far too large to enter Falmouth docks, whilst the latter's dry docks would be used by many vessels from the St. Just wharves.[17]

Amidst all this enthusiasm, only one individual, a Mr. J. Durgy, wrote to the *Packet*, pointing out that 'no one as yet has publicly paid the tribute of a sigh to the beauty which will be destroyed when the scheme is carried into effect... Certainly there is a mysterious quiet about the place. This influence centres about the ancient church, which stands on a little subsidiary creek of its own, and which, at the proper season, is surrounded by a great show of roses'. Mr. Durgy went on to assert that the land at St. Just reaped the advantage of earlier crops - 'they start harvest there fully a fortnight before the farms on the opposite side of the harbour' - and 'instead of the furze blossom and the dog rose, navvies' huts will arise in all their beauty, and the ancient peace will be broken by the shriek of railway whistles; there will probably be a picture palace'.[18]

Writing in the *Daily Mail*, Mr. C. Fox Smith stated:

'Falmouth is practically the first harbour of importance on the South Coast for ships bound up the Channel, and during the war that circumstance, as well as the closing of the ports of Plymouth and Southampton to mercantile traffic, has brought a crowd of shipping in the Roads, including many a lame duck which might just as well have been drydocked on the spot had accommodation been available... . While it should not be forgotten that the present activity is largely due to abnormal conditions, and may or may not survive the circumstances which created it, it seems rational to make use of the natural advantages offered by the St. Just site, should an extension of the port be necessary, rather than to extend the old harbour of Falmouth... . Against the advantages of the scheme must be set two or three decided drawbacks. One of these is the dangerous character of the coastline in the vicinity, which is full of perils in foggy or stormy weather. A more important consideration from the commercial point of view is its remoteness from London and from industrial centres, as well as the absence of any coal-producing and manufacturing areas within a reasonable radius. Like all such projects, it is regarded with mixed feelings. Naturally, local business people and property owners hail it with enthusiasm. Falmouth no less naturally is inclined to look a little askance; while those who know the lovely little church of St. Just-in-Roseland, with its grey old tower set amid stately trees and tropical shrubs, and its beautiful graveyard sloping steeply down to the waters of St. Just Creek, cannot but sigh to think of its peace being broken by the raucous note of the steam whistle, the grinding and clanking of winch and derrick, and the deafening sound of rivetters at work'.[19]

A Canadian newspaper, the *Toronto Star*, reported that the final plans made provision for 40,000 feet of deep water wharves with a depth of 44 feet alongside at low water and a 1,100 feet dry dock, and that as the British government looked upon Falmouth as 'one of the finest sites for a terminal port and port of call in the United Kingdom', it was likely that the government would see that the full plan was implemented.[20]

When the draft bill was before the House of Lords, it was argued for the promoters that the inexorable trend was for vessels to grow larger, and that St. Just could already accommodate the largest foreseeable ships, whilst all other ports in the United Kingdom would require expensive deepening for this to be the case. It was also pointed out that vessels sailing from Halifax, Nova Scotia, or New York were 153 nautical miles nearer to Falmouth than they were to Southampton, where an eight mile channel with a maximum depth of 35 feet had to be navigated, and that at Liverpool there were 13 miles of river to navigate before ships reached the docks, which had a depth at low tide of only 23 feet. It followed from this, or so it was argued, that St. Just should have a monopoly of the trade carried on by steamers of larger draft where owners were anxious to shorten the length of the voyage and avoid delay.[21]

In September 1919, it was reported that 'operations preliminary to the construction of the docks have already begun' and that for all practical purposes the docks and railway should be in full use two years hence'.[22] America was thought to be planning two new huge liners, bigger than anything then in service, and that since American capital was to be invested in the St. Just scheme, it would follow that these 'Atlantic monsters' would naturally use Falmouth as their British destination.[23] However, by the end of 1919, the first suggestions of doubt were appearing, not due to anything lacking in the merits of the scheme itself, but because of the claims, much canvassed, of the existing naval ports to be entitled to develop into mercantile trade, and the lack of enthusiasm of the Great Western Railway towards the construction of the new line. In particular, Plymouth was looking after its own interests, its representatives meeting the Prime Minister to 'point to their two main line railways and to their port facilities', enabling passengers to be in London within four hours after disembarking, and making the bull point that their city's facilities were already in place, whilst those at Falmouth were still on the drawing board. As the *Packet* put it, 'everything will depend upon the financial prospects, and whether the passing of the St. Just Bill can today, under the existing circumstances, procure the large amount of money that is necessary'.[24]

There indeed was the rub. With the Admiralty not interested in developing Falmouth into a permanent naval base, and therefore no government money being available, the existing naval bases extolling their own merits when it came to mercantile expansion, and the Great Western having no wish to put in the line to St. Just, the possibility of attracting vast American finance for the scheme became increasingly remote. The silver lining to the cloud of despondency caused by the gradual dissolution of the hopes that Falmouth would become one of England's premier ports is that future generations are still able to enjoy one of the loveliest unspoilt harbours of the world.

NOTES

[1] *The Submarine Service, 1900-1918*, Nicholas Lambert (ed.), Navy Records Society, 2001. Pp226-229

[2] Ibid., p232

[3] FP,10.3.1916, p4

[4] FP, 5.5.1916

[5] FP, 8.6.1917, p2

[6] FP, 8.6.1917, p4

[7] WMN, reprinted in FP, 4.1.1918

[8] FP, 8.3.1918, p4

[9] FP, 14.6.1918

[10] WB, 16.12.1917, p4

[11] WB, 23.5.1918, p7

[12] WB, 6.12.1917, p4
[13] WB, 3.6.1918, p2
[14] WB, 13.6.1918, p4
[15] FP, 23.1.1914, p5
[16] FP, 16.5.1919, p4
[17] WB, 16.1.1919, p3
[18] FP, 13.6.1919, p6

[19] *Daily Mail*, 2.7.1919, reprinted in FP, 4.7.1919, p5
[20] *Toronto Star,* 28.6.1919, as reprinted in WB, 29.8.1919, p4
[21] WB, 1.5.1919, p4
[22] WB, 22.9.1919, p2
[23] WB, 31.7.1919, p4
[24] WB, 13.11.1919

CHAPTER XV

'THERE'S A LONG ROAD A'WINDING' - 1918

'Scores of steamers' whistle and sirens' welcomed in the New Year in Falmouth. 'The hooting did not cease until ten minutes to one, much to the discomfort of some people, but to the delight of others, who looked upon the demonstration as a happy augury for 1918'.[1] Perhaps the sight of a seal sleeping on the rocks opposite the Falmouth Hotel was also thought to augur well for the fifth year of war.[2]

The local MP, Major C.S. Goldman, made a speech in January at the local Conservative Club. He reviewed the military situation, balancing the disappointments of 1917, the collapse of Russia, defeats suffered by Italy, the lack of spectacular gains on the Western Front, and the danger caused by the U-boat campaign, with the successes in Germany's African colonies, in Mesopotamia, 'the capture of the Holy Land by our gallant troops', the war weariness in Austria-Hungary, Bulgaria and Turkey and, above all, the entry of the United States into the war. Major Goldman did not deny that there was war weariness in this country as well, and that the war had increased the nation's debt from £700,000,000 in 1914 to £5,700,000,000 four years later, but with American industrial and financial muscle the tide had turned inexorably against Germany, whose imperative desire it was to have an early peace. He went on to warn his audience that 'the party truce was fast disappearing', as politicians looked to the world after the war, and that the Labour Party was particularly active in spreading its message and influence in all directions, but particularly in the teaching profession. It was necessary for his party, the Conservatives, to formulate a programme for peace, whilst at the same time keeping 'their minds firmly fixed on the War'. He surmised that many of the soldiers returning home after the war would seek new lives in the Dominions and colonies overseas, but for those who wanted to stay in this country new and healthy housing must be built - 'the slum must disappear like an ugly nightmare'. Priority must also be given to education, and 'the whole status of the teaching profession must undergo a complete change'. A new relationship between employers and labour was required 'to prevent the unhappy misunderstandings and conflicts of the past'. Major Goldman also drew attention to the huge financial difficulties caused by the war indebtedness, together with the inevitable demands 'on the national exchequer for social, educational and commercial reconstruction', but he stopped short of suggesting how these problems were to be overcome.[3] Goldman represented a constituency consisting of Falmouth and Penryn, known as the United Borough, but as a result of the deliberations of the Boundary Commission this small constituency was in future elections to be added to that of Truro and St. Austell.[4]

Goldman's reference to the 'status of the teaching profession' was apposite, as that profession in Falmouth was extremely unhappy. The *Packet*, which by early 1918 had been reduced in size because of paper restrictions and its price had risen from 1d to 1½d, acknowledged that teachers in Falmouth 'had a real grievance' over their rate of pay. A comparison was made with salaries in Penzance, as follows:

Male Head teachers - Falmouth - £170 - Penzance - £193
Female Heads - Falmouth - £96 - Penzance - £114
Male teachers - Falmouth - £94 - Penzance - £104
Female teachers - Falmouth - £70 - Penzance - £85

Of the 124 borough committees throughout the country, Falmouth came 10th from bottom in rates of pay as regards male heads, 3rd from bottom as regards female heads, 16th from bottom as regards male teachers and 2nd from bottom as regards female teachers.[5] Teachers in all Falmouth schools tendered their resignations over the issue, but these were refused by the Corporation who agreed to pay teachers 'from 25th December the same salaries as they would now or in the future receive under the county scale for similar services'. It would seem, therefore, that there was one scale for teachers employed by the county, and another, lower, scale for those employed by the borough, and that in future Falmouth teachers were to receive the higher county scale of pay. This would add £864 per year to the rates, and this figure would increase year by year, but all members of the Corporation felt that they had no option but to vote in favour.[6]

The Medical Officer of the Falmouth and Truro Port Sanitary Authority reported that he had examined 281 vessels in 1917, and that the predominate disease was malaria. However, the massive use of the port during the wartime years was evidenced by the report of the sanitary inspector, who had examined 2766 vessels, of which 1616 were British.[7]

The last great assault of the German Army in March 1918, which became known as the Kaiser's Battle, was reported fully in the *Packet*, under the heading, 'The Greatest Battle in History'.[8] There was no thought that the war could be over in a matter of months; on the contrary, an army chaplain wrote home from France, 'Quite frankly, I don't see any end for the war under nine or ten years, unless we break - which to the proud Englishman is unthinkable'.[9] By contrast, the treaty of Brest-Litovsk, by which Germany imposed draconian terms on the new Russian Bolshevik government, and ended Russian participation in the war, received minimal attention in the *Packet*, simply a small paragraph at the foot of page 4. 'So ends the great farce. There is not apparently to be even the formality of a treaty. Presumably Germany is to take all she has a mind to, or can carry away'.[10]

War wounded servicemen are entertained to a bowls match at the Recreation Ground 1918

It is not clear how far the jurisdiction of the local coroner extended, but cases were reported of inquests held on seamen lost at sea as a result of enemy action. At one such inquest on seamen killed when their ship was torpedoed, the jury protested against a local pub owner, who was not named, who refused hospitality to survivors from this ship because they were coloured. The jury 'strongly condemned such treatment of brave men who were facing peril in order to supply the country with food and other supplies', and asked the captain, who had been torpedoed five times, to convey their sentiments to his crew. The jury also asked the coroner to bring to the notice of the proper authorities their opinion that no British subjects of enemy origin should be allowed to reside on the sea coast.[11]

War or no war, life had to go on and mundane transactions such as the sale of houses were reported in the *Packet*. No. 24 Florence Terrace was sold for £527, and 85 Marlborough Road for £445.[12] 'The Romance of David Lloyd George' was showing at St. George's Hall, although one assumes that this had little to do with the Prime Minister's notorious love life.[13] Under the heading, 'The Nobleman and the Policeman', the *Packet* reported the case of Lord Drumlanrig who was brought before the magistrates charged with riding a motorcycle without a licence. 'His Lordship had been in France for three years (except when he came home suffering from wounds) and was allowed to go where he liked without any licence. When he came home he thought that the same procedure applied, and it did not occur to him that a civil licence was necessary for riding a military bicycle in pursuance of his military duties'. However, one feels that the real reason why this very insignificant case came to court was because, in the words of Superintendent Nicholls, 'Lord Drumlanrig treated the sergeant in anything but a courteous way; he was snubbed because he was a common policeman and of inferior social position'. The noble lord then said that he had not the slightest intention of being in any way discourteous to the sergeant - 'being a gentleman himself, he does not want to be discourteous to anyone who happens to hold an inferior position socially'. The bench considered that a fine of 5s met the case.[14]

At the annual meeting of the River Fal Steamship Company, a member suggested the erection of glass screens to protect passengers in stormy weather, describing a trip when 'everyone was shivering like wet dogs'. What seems a reasonable and relatively inexpensive improvement was turned down on account of the cost, and also due to the somewhat surreal assertion that glass screens would prevent the towing of schooners.[15]

Lord Claude Hamilton gave an address to the Falmouth Women's Social Institute. Having outlined the reasons for going to war, being treaty obligations to Belgium and a desire to help France, he went on to assert that there could be no peace until Germany had been utterly defeated, which would happen with the aid of the American forces now pouring into France. Whilst he had been against women suffrage, he now recognised that the enormous contribution of women during the war entitled them to the vote. The question then arose, how would they use their vote? 'In a place like the Falmouth district they were inclined to take too narrow and local a view of their responsibility. They must not think locally, they must think imperially. They must consider that they are part and parcel of a great and glorious empire and every vote given must necessarily have its effect on the control of the whole of the empire'. Social matters such as improvement of housing for the working class were vital, as were higher wages for the artisan, and this would mean heavy taxation in the medium term but would result in 'increased comfort all round'.[16]

The children from the various schools gathered on the Moor to celebrate Empire Day. The Mayor informed them that this was held on 24th May, being the birthday of Queen Victoria, under whose rule 'the Empire grew to its present greatness'. Canon King told the children that 'the Empire is based on three principles - self government, self-support, self-defence, and as long as these principles could be properly carried out, it would continue to stand for all that is good and noble'. The chairman of the education committee, Mr. C. Spargo, then informed the children that Britain 'stood on a pedestal of honour and glory compared with the race of Huns who glorified in rape and rapine, savagery and slaughter' and that Christian ministers throughout the Empire supported the British struggle 'against the forces of hell now ranged against them'.[17] Canon King's delicate health forced his resignation in July 1918, but before it could take effect, he died the following month; he was extremely popular in the town, and what may seem to the present day reader as his extremely militant, not to say jingoistic, views, he was simply expressing the sentiments of the vast majority of his parishioners.

The cost of postage of a letter had remained at one penny since 1840, and continued at this rate for letters to men at the front, but for everyone else the cost went up to $1\frac{1}{2}$d in June 1918.[18]

There were, on the face of it, extraordinary variations in the purchase of National War Bonds between various Cornish towns. Way out in front in June 1918 was Penzance, with a population of 13,500, which had purchased bonds in the preceding 34 weeks totalling £304,515. In the same period, Falmouth, with a population of 13,100, could only manage £135,347. Equally odd is the contrast between Camborne and Redruth; the former with a population of 15,800 could only manage £55,536, while Redruth, with a population of only 10,800, purchased an astonishing £278,426. The figures suggest far greater wealth in Penzance compared with Falmouth, and even more so in Redruth compared with its less fortunate neighbour.[19] By 1918, the 15,800 in Camborne were served by only two doctors as a result of war service.[20] Falmouth held a 'Weapons Week' from 2nd to 8th July 1918. The aim was to raise money to build five tanks, which then cost £5,000 each, on which would be inscribed the name of the town.[21] In the event, the final figure raised fell rather short of that hoped for, at £17,447, but it still seems a considerable sum for a small town to raise, especially having regard to all the other war orientated funds to which the public were asked to subscribe.[22]

The various strata of social class were never far from the surface of everyday life, and reports of weddings were carefully graded in the local press, starting on the lowest rung as 'pretty', 'very pretty' and 'exceedingly pretty', moving up to 'interesting' and finally to 'fashionable'. Concerns about the behaviour of the young were as prevalent then as they are now; a Wesleyan minister was shocked by the 'appalling amount of sexual immorality in Cornwall amongst young people in their teens'.[23] At the other end of the age scale, the Old Age Pensions Committee was busy - one applicant received 5s a week, one 4s, and a third refused on the grounds that his income exceeded £31.10.0 a year.[24]

The question of what form a war memorial should take began to occupy the minds of local people in the summer of 1918. At a public meeting, the general feeling was that, whilst there should be some form of monument, the main memorial should be something of benefit to the town, and the popular choice was a children's ward at the hospital. A committee was formed to consider the matter, which reported to a further public meeting, at which it was agreed that the memorial should be a monument and a children's ward.[25]

An example of the considerably more robust attitude, than is prevalent today amongst the establishment, to an Englishman's home being his castle, was the case of a clergyman, who killed an intruder by suffocating him. The coroner exonerated him from all blame since 'he had a right to protect his own property', and no charges were brought against him.[26]

An appeal in the town for books, to be donated to be sent to soldiers overseas, listed 'the names of writers dear to soldiers - O. Henry, Kipling, Dumas, Nat Gould, the author of Sexton Blake, Rex Beard, Jack London'. Also handbooks on 'oil engines, international law, electricity, philosophy, chicken farming, gardening, boxing, ferrets, wood carving, history of musicians etc'.[27] A young officer wrote home to his parents from the front, 'last night I read a novel of Nat Gould. Do you read Nat Gould? His books literally sell by millions. I had difficulty in finding this particular volume, as my servant had pinched it and it was rapidly going the rounds of the section'.[28] His brother, also an officer at the front, gave a somewhat unexpected insight into life in the trenches:

'You would be surprised if you saw how well we live in the trenches. We have always four courses at dinner. At breakfast we have porridge, eggs and bacon, tea and coffee; at lunch roast meat and a pudding; at tea, jam, bread and butter, and a cake from some home parcel; and at dinner, soup, meat, sweet and savoury. For drinks we have red and white wine and whiskey. Whisky has been very difficult to obtain lately. We always finish up at night with hot rum punch, a really excellent beverage I assure you for these bitter nights'.[29]

There were more people on holiday in Cornwall in August 1918 than at any time since the war began. Money was plentiful for hundreds of thousands on high wages, and many had not taken a holiday for four years. As the visitors flooded into Falmouth, it was not always easy to feed them, because although they brought their ration coupons with them, some of the food stuffs were in short supply.[30] However, it was a bumper year for blackberries, '350 tons had been secured in Cornwall for the nation'.[31]

Captain and Mrs. Bosanquet of Falmouth were drowned when their liner, *Galway Castle*, was torpedoed, but their nine month old baby survived, due to a lady passenger who kept hold of the child when clinging to a raft 'repeatedly swept by waves'. She 'devoted what she could of her scanty attire towards protecting the baby'.[32]

As if the civilian population had not enough to contend with, by the autumn of 1918 'Spanish flu' began to sweep the country, and Falmouth was not spared - deaths from this epidemic, which was to kill world wide four times as many as the total casualties of the war, were reported in the *Packet* each week in late 1918. Schools had to close to reduce the risk of infection, and church attendances dropped as people feared catching the infection. There was no known cure, so there was little that the doctors could do. A strange aspect of the infection was that it seemed to attack the young and healthy more than the usual victims of an epidemic, the poor and old. Upwards of 230,000 people in the country died from 'the Spanish Lady' before the epidemic finally abated in the spring of 1919.[33]

Rabies still existed in Cornwall; in 1918 there were 58 suspected cases of rabies, of which 17 were definitely confirmed, and it was a criminal offence to allow a dog to stray from the owner's premises without a muzzle.[34] No dog could be moved out of Cornwall, and someone who did so was heavily fined. One doubts if the RSPCA today would endorse the view of their local inspector then, who thought that some good came out of the rabies outbreak, because 'it got rid of a large number of dogs they did not want to see hanging around the streets'.[35]

The normal decorum of mayor choosing was somewhat ruffled in November 1918, when Councillor C. Spargo was elected Mayor. The outgoing mayor, C. Rusden, was very aggrieved that he had not been given a second term in office, claiming that his removal had been 'engineered' by a cabal.[36]

It must have seemed to the people of Falmouth that peace arrived all of a rush in November 1918, after over four long years of war. Only a short time before, an officer wrote home from the front: 'If only I could give to our grandchildren and great-grandchildren some picture - a true picture - of what this war is like - its wonderful sacrifice, but its equally wonderful brutality - its grandeur and nobility, but its equally great selfishness and self-seeking; its intense excitement, but its long boredom and monotony; the extraordinary efficiency and the marvellous inefficiency of the Army; the contrasts of this kind could be numbered by the score'.[37] Even as late as the 7th November, another officer wrote home, 'We all, except the Staff Officers who don't see anything of the fighting or of the morale of the Germans, anticipate another six months of fighting at least'.[38]

But, at last, came the eleventh hour of the eleventh day of the eleventh month.

NOTES

[1] FP, 4.1.1918, p2
[2] FP, 4.1.1918, p2
[3] FP, 11.1.1918, p3
[4] FP, 4.1.1918
[5] FP, 1.3.1918, p4
[6] FP, 15.3.1918, p3
[7] FP, 29.3.1918, p2
[8] FP, 29.3.1918, p3
[9] *The Bickersteth Diaries*, ibid., p257
[10] FP, 15.2.1918, p4
[11] WB, 23.5.1918, p3
[12] FP, 17.5.1918, p2
[13] FP, 2.3.1918, p2
[14] FP, 3.5.1918, p4
[15] WB, 16.5.1918, p7
[16] FP, 24.5.1918, p4
[17] FP, 31.5.1918, p4
[18] WB, 6.6.1918, p7
[19] WB, 6.6.1918, p7
[20] FP, 26.7.1918, p4
[21] FP, 21.6.1918, p2
[22] FP, 19.7.1918, p2
[23] WB, 13.6.1918, p4
[24] FP, 2.8.1918, p2
[25] FP, 21.6.1918, p4 & 26.7.1918, p3
[26] FP, 19.7.1918, p2
[27] FP, 19.7.1918, p3
[28] *The Bickersteth Diaries*, ibid., p212
[29] Ibid., p155
[30] WB, 19.8.1918, p2
[31] FP, 4.10.1918, p2
[32] FP, 20.9.1918, p4
[33] *All Quiet On The Home Front*, ibid., p285
[34] FP, 13.12.1918, p3
[35] WB, 3.4.1919, p5
[36] FP, 15.11.1918, p3
[37] *The Bickersteth Diaries*, ibid., p143
[38] Ibid., p295

CHAPTER XVI

THE ARMISTICE

The *Packet* described the reaction to the news of the Armistice thus:

'It's Peace! It's Peace!! It's Peace!!! Such were the exclamations of hundreds of persons in Falmouth about 9.10 on Monday morning when the sirens and the hooters of the minesweepers and the other steamers in the harbour, and the bells on the various coasting vessels all joined in announcing the glad tidings. People knew what the hooting meant. They had been accustomed to hearing the shrieking of the sirens on a watch night bidding adieu to the old year and welcoming in the new, and they were certain that there was only one meaning to Monday morning's outburst, and that was that the Armistice had been signed. Mothers, sisters and sweethearts cried with joy, and even some strong men wept when they thought what it meant to their boys on the battlefields and in the prisoners' camps. It was washing day in most homes, but few cared for this. Away went the washing, and in a surprisingly short time hundreds of people were rushing to the town to glean further tidings. Meanwhile a veritable pandemonium prevailed, for the number of ships' sirens was increased as the various patrol and other vessels arrived one by one. Added to this was the powerful siren at the electric works and the hooter at the Foundry.

Falmouth heard the news quite two hours earlier than most towns in the country, for the Naval officials had received the intelligence which soon spread. People began to pour into the streets, which were quickly filled with a jostling, jubilant crowd. They were considerably added to in a few minutes by the employees from the Falmouth Foundry and Docks, who came trooping through the town singing and cheering to their hearts' content. Meanwhile, flags, streamers and bunting of all descriptions were being draped on shop fronts and being hung across the streets, and in an incredibly short space of time the main thoroughfare presented a remarkably gay appearance. Repeated reports were heard in the harbour, and as the crowds surged onto the various quays a delightful scene was revealed. Red, blue and green rockets were bursting high in the air, and every vessel both large and small was adorned in a mass of flags and bunting. The sirens kept up a perpetual din, and boats leaving the various craft at anchor gave the impression of bunches of excited human arms wildly waving. Many of the businesses had by this time closed and various bizarre figures appeared in the crowd, which was increasing at every moment. Amongst these was an old baker, who, with the aid of a pair of goggles, a top hat and a Union Jack to the extremity of which was tied a bunch of leeks, presented a most fantastic sight, and caused much merriment. The beating of drums could now be heard, and the people commenced to move towards Market Strand, from which direction the sound proceeded. Coming down the High Street was an apparently endless stream of soldiers, belonging to the Rifle Brigade, marching four deep and interspersed with WAACs, land workers, etc. The procession was headed by the Rifle Brigade bugle band, but there were, at intervals in it, sundry other bands of considerable power, laudable originality, but doubtful melody, consisting of tin pans, saucepans, bones, mouth organs etc, which highly amused the onlookers and also, to join by appearances, the performers. Conspicuous in the centre of the procession was Rifleman Shambrook, whose costume consisted of a butcher's smock and apron over his regimentals. The military were followed by the Salvation Army band, rendering such music as 'Men of Harlech', 'Rule Britannia' and other patriotic airs, and the members deserve much praise for their services in this and many other respects. The Salvation Army did not leave the main street, but the soldiers continued down

Bar Terrace, and so around the Marine Drive, and back via Fenwick Road and Melville Road. As the Royal Engineer barracks was passed, another 'band' emerged, which had very evidently commandeered every drum in the place. Rattles also came into prominence and the noise increased to an alarming pitch. The sirens and hooters had not ceased blowing for a moment, and an aeroplane was seen in the distance. The occupants evidently saw the line of khaki winding along by the sea, and after some dizzy circling in order to get lower, it swooped along at no great distance above the heads of the moving column. Several times it returned and the sight was a very pretty one. Those of the patients at the Pendennis Military Hospital who were able to go out, were lined just behind the low hedge, together with the staff, and were cheered to the echo by the soldiers in the road.

During the afternoon all ranks of the Army might be seen parading the streets arm-in-arm, and the happy faces proved the relief and satisfaction afforded by allowing the pent-up feelings of four years to have full play. Motor cars and lorries full of smiling Tommies and Jack Tars passed through the streets and when darkness set in the crowds were still in evidence. Fairy lamps and various forms of illumination were to be seen in windows and across roads, whilst very pretty effects were obtained in the harbour by the burning of flares of all colours and the firing off of rockets. Squibs and 'jumpers' were the order of the day among the rising generation, and miniature displays of fireworks took place at every street corner.

It was pleasing to note that during all the rejoicing and jubilation that took place there was very little drunkenness or rowdyism, and this is something on which the men of the Forces and the inhabitants generally are to be complimented in no stinted terms. When at last Falmouthians retired to rest, they were astonished to hear several sirens and hooters that had taken such a prominent part in the morning's proceedings, recommence anew, and until close upon midnight the din from the harbour continued. Rockets were also fired. After that, all was quiet, and one of the most eventful days in the town's history had drawn to a close'.[1]

The Armistice was not a day of celebration for all. Mr. and Mrs. Wilson of Penwerris Terrace were told that their son, William, had been killed in action four days earlier.[2] Of the two thousand plus men from Falmouth who had served in the armed services, ten per cent had lost their lives and a much larger percentage had been wounded, many to the extent that they could no longer work.[3] A Thanksgiving service held in the Cathedral for the county as a whole was much criticised in letters to the press, being described as 'cold, formal and stereotyped as it could be', no General Thanksgiving, no celebratory hymns such as 'Now Thank We All Our God', an anthem by the choir 'which no one wanted to hear' and large numbers of the congregation being unable to hear the Bishop's words.

Two days after the news of the Armistice, the celebrations continued with 'a monster Naval, Military and civilian torchlight procession'. Among those taking part were the Rifle Brigade, men from the Naval Base and from American ships then in the harbour, men from the RAF and 'also members of the WAACs, Women's Land Army etc., looking delightful in the ruddy glare of innumerable torches carried by the men'. The procession eventually arrived at the Moor, where 'the Mayor addressed an immense audience, and on his own behalf, and on behalf of the inhabitants generally, thanked Sir Norman Murray for making the event such a great success. That gentleman was serving in the Australian forces (he had been twice wounded) and was doing all that lay in his power to show his loyalty to the country by arranging such events as that, and organising all kinds of charitable work'. The Mayor then went on to demand the trial and execution of the Kaiser.[5] It later transpired that 'Sir' Norman was a confidence trickster with a string of convictions behind him - 'during the past 23 years the all-round humbug and shallow-pated egotist has spent something like 18 years in the gaols of every Australian state except Western Australia'. He seems to have specialised in extracting money posing as a parson, and bigamously marrying women thought to be wealthy.[6]

In December 1918, the U101 was brought to Falmouth and was moored alongside the Prince of Wales Pier, and was opened to the public at 1s each. It was described as 'the most modern type of submarine used by the Germans in their piratical warfare'.[7]

When the German fleet surrendered to the British in 1918, 176 U-boats were taken to Harwich. Some were sent to be put on display in British ports, and nine accompanied by a supply ship were towed to Falmouth, although one sank on the way. Two more were 'tested to destruction' in Falmouth Bay, and the remaining six were all thrown up on the rocks on the western side of Pendennis Point in a severe storm in March or April 1921. They were then dragged up on to a tidal rock platform by the depot ship, *Cyklops* 'so as not to be a danger to shipping, and there they lay, a tourist attraction and playground for local youth until the Second World War', when they were broken up, but the bare skeletons can still be seen at very low spring tides.[8]

With the ending of hostilities, a general election, postponed during the war, could be held. From the reign of Queen Mary, 1552-1558, Falmouth had returned two members of parliament. It was joined with Penryn by the Great Reform Act of 1832, and Flushing was added to the constituency in 1868, since which date it had returned one member.[9] However, the Boundary Commission greatly altered the Cornish constituencies in time for what became known as the 'Khaki Election' in December 1918, and the former United Borough constituency formed part of a much larger one, with Truro and St. Austell. Unlike 1945, after the defeat of Hitler, party politics did not return to the pre-war status quo. The Liberal Party split between adherents of the Prime Minister, Lloyd George, who wanted to

German Submarines ashore at Falmouth

109

German Submarines dumped on Castle Beach

Submarine lifting vessel, 'Cyklops'.

continue the wartime coalition with the Conservatives, and those of the former Prime Minister, Asquith, who wanted an end to coalition rule. The Coalition candidate in the new constituency which included Falmouth, Sir Edward Nicholl, a commander RNR and a native of Redruth, won the seat, with a slim majority of 235 over the Asquithian Liberal, Sir Arthur Carkeek. The total electorate was 35,000 of which 19,952 voted, and included in the figure of 35,000 were 8,000 serving in the forces, of which only 2,200 voted. 'It is doubtful if there has ever been a parliamentary election at which so much apathy has been shown'.[10] There was much speculation as to why this should have been so, and one explanation put forward was that many Liberals away in the forces did not want to vote against Lloyd George, who they greatly respected, but could not bring themselves to vote for a coalition which included the Conservatives. Another possibility put forward by the *Briton* was that the Unionists or Conservatives, who supported the continuation of the coalition government, were much better organised than the Liberals, and whilst they got out their vote in great numbers, the Liberals did not.[11] Sir Arthur Carkeek had no doubt as to the reason for his defeat; in his view, the name of Lloyd George heading the Coalition ticket accounted for at least one third of the votes cast for the winners.[12]

This was the first election in which women were allowed to vote, and as a result the total Cornish electorate went up from 83,571 to 152,132.[13] In the constituency which included Falmouth, 15,486 women were on the electoral roll, but there is no information as to the numbers who exercised their right to vote. What is perhaps surprising at first sight is that no controversy was reported in the local press over this momentous extension of the franchise. It appears to have been generally accepted that the huge contribution of women to the war effort fully entitled them to an equal share with men in deciding on the country's rulers.

One of the planks of Nicholls's election manifesto was the provision of new housing by the State to replace the existing slums in Falmouth, a place which in his opinion 'had every prospect of a great future before it, and in twenty years the population ought to increase from 13,000 to 30,000'.[14] However, his main concern was to insist upon the payment by Germany of reparations to cover the whole cost of the war. In April 1919, he told the House of Commons that his career as an MP was likely to be a very short one, as he would have to resign if Lloyd George did not see that Germany was made responsible for the whole cost of the conflict. In his speech, Sir Edward quoted the staggering figure of 22,750,000 tons of shipping sunk by Germany, and the loss of 17,000 men in the mercantile marine - 'If this country does not get an indemnity, we shall want to know the reason why, and the life of this Government will be a very short one'.[15]

Lieutenant Luard, son of Major and Mrs. Luard of Woodlane, was a prisoner of war in Germany, and he described what happened when the Armistice was signed and the Kaiser abdicated. 'The revolution proved a very quiet affair. The officers threw away their uniforms and donned civilian attire. The commandant of the camp who happened to be away at the time refused to obey the behests of the Socialist Party, returned to the camp and asked to be admitted to his old post. He had to flee to save his life and one of the old officers was appointed in his stead. The prisoners were then allowed to go for walks under the charge of a guard, and later they were allowed out on parole. The German towns were decorated with flags in honour of the homecoming of the 'victorious troops'!' The British prisoners of war were free to go where they chose, the cafes, theatres etc., being open to them. On one occasion Lieutenant Luard visited a theatre and witnessed a production of *Hamlet*. Such was the freedom granted to British officers that they could have easily crossed the Rhine and have gained their freedom, but they were reminded by their seniors that they were on parole and that their honour was being trusted. In Germany, Lieutenant Luard stated that rubber was unprocurable, and wonderful results were achieved by the use of paper and wood. Boots were made of those materials, for no leather could be obtained; a pair of English boots would realise £20. The Germans would also give ten shillings for half of a twopenny cake of English soap.[16]

NOTES

[1] FP, 15.11.1918

[2] FP, 22.11.1918, p3

[3] FP, 14.11.1919, p5

[4] WB, 14.11.1918, p5

[5] FP, 22.11.1918, p3

[6] *Melbourne Truth,* 1.3.1919, as reprinted in the FP, 16.5.1919, p4

[7] FP, 20.12.1918, p2

[8] Peter Gilson, FP, 15.1.1998

[9] WB, 2.1.1919, p4

[10] WB, 2.1.1919, p5

[11] WB, 30.12.1918, p2

[12] WB, 2.1.1919, p5

[13] WB, 4.7.1918, p3

[14] FP, 22.11.1918, p3

[15] WB, 3.4.1919, p5

[16] FP, 13.12.1918, p3

CHAPTER XVII

THE RETURN OF PEACE

The dawn of 1919 was greeted with joy and relief. A great cloud had been lifted, although there can have been few families who had not been seared by the casualties of war. There had to be two Victory Balls held in January at the Princess Pavilion, such was the demand for tickets, priced at 5s for a double ticket and 3s 6d for a single.[1] In March, a contingent from the Italian Navy was in Falmouth, escorting a flotilla of former German U-boats to Italy for exhibition purposes. The officers gave a ball at the Pavilion, and 'no effort was spared to make the building look as picturesque as possible... As each lady guest arrived, she was presented with a choice bouquet of carnations and lilies of the valley, which was tied with the Italian colours'.[2] The wife of Private Charles Broom of Falmouth had been told in April 1918 that her husband had been killed in action. In fact, he had been wounded and captured, and arrived back in Falmouth in January. 'I nearly fell down with joy' was the response of Mrs. Broom.[3]

The War Hospital Supply Depot closed in February 1919, having made a total of 36,900 articles.[4] The War Memorial Committee had to postpone the creation of a children's ward at the hospital 'because of building difficulties', but proceeded with a granite Cornish cross 'upon a pedestal sufficiently large to bear the names of all those who have lost their lives in the War', the height to be about 36 feet. A further £200 had to be raised to pay for this memorial.[5]

Whilst the men started to come home from the armed forces, many had to spend up to a year or more after the Armistice in the services. Under the heading 'A Sailor's Grumble', a native of Falmouth serving in the eastern Mediterranean wrote to the *Packet*, pointing out that whilst letters and parcels had been sent to Falmouthians serving in the United Kingdom, those serving abroad seem to have been forgotten, as in three and a half years he and others serving with him had received no letters or parcels, except from relations. 'The least the natives of Falmouth could have done was to send a Christmas greeting, but we have the consolation that we will not have to acknowledge and thank our townsmen when we do reach Blighty'.[6] This 'grumble' was backed up by subsequent letters along the same lines from a sailor serving with the Grand Fleet and a soldier in France. [7]

In March 1919, the traditional rivalry on the rugby field between Falmouth and Penryn recommenced, with Falmouth the narrow winners. 'The game reminded rugby enthusiasts of those titanic struggles which used to take place between the fifteens a score of years ago, when no referee in Cornwall was thought impartial enough to take charge of the matches and an official had to be requisitioned from Devon'.[8] Punctuality does not seem to have been a strong suit with rugby teams, because there were complaints that rugby matches at the Recreation Ground, advertised to start at 3.15pm, often did not actually kick off until after 4.00, 'causing the spectators to suffer from frost bitten toes and blue noses'.[9] In May, Cornwall appeared to have won a momentous victory over New Zealand by 16 points to 11, having previously lost narrowly to Australia, but closer examination shows that the visiting teams were drawn from Antipodean servicemen who happened to be in this country at the time.[10] Soccer was slower to get off the ground after the war in Falmouth, the reason put forth for this being the number of players still away in the forces.[11]

To be an aviator in those days, when the 'nanny state' was unknown, really did bestow the freedom of the skies, and Captain Wilfred Cox MC 'testing a new machine, fitted with a 400 hp Liberty engine', and reaching a speed of 130mph, flew low over Falmouth and dropped a letter addressed to his parents within 100 yards of their home, 'Kinbrae', and then went on to Coverack where his wife was staying and did the same.[12]

The depth of anti-German feeling resulted in persons raising the question whether the eagle should be removed from the town s coat of arms in view of its German connections. More sensible voices pointed out that Killigrew meant 'a grove of eagles' and that the eagle was just as much a British bird as a German. 'Instead of Falmouthians thinking of abolishing the eagle from their coat of arms, it is up to them to petition the Big Four to make it a condition of peace that Germany be no longer allowed to employ it as her device'.[13] A German U-boat commander, Capt. Kieswetter, had been apprehended in Falmouth in May on a ship bound for Holland, and accused of war crimes, including attacking hospital ships. He had been lodged in the Tower of London, but was released in August 1919 without charge. The *Packet* was incensed - 'Such folly increases the scepticism as to whether any German criminals will ever be put on trial'.[14]

The Medical Officer of Health, Dr. Gregor, presented his annual report on the health of Falmouth in May. Infant mortality had risen again 'to an alarming extent', and it was noted that 14 of the 22 deaths of infants had occurred 'in the congested areas of the town'. It seems that boys were more susceptible to insanitary conditions than girls, as 19 of the 22 deaths were of boys. The natural decrease in the population amounted to 33 - deaths, 235, births 202 - and it was only the second time in ten years that deaths had exceeded births. The deaths included 21 from the great influenza epidemic sweeping the country, but in addition there were 19 deaths of sailors as a result of enemy action. 'With such figures before us, and when such a large proportion of our manhood has either been killed or maimed, there is only one rational method of dealing with such a situation, and that is to use every means known to raise the standard of public health in the borough and to conserve our infant life. Unless the position is attacked in a clear and statesmanlike fashion from every point, the result will be ill health, physical deterioration, and consequent loss of economic power'. There had been an epidemic of measles, 182 cases being reported, resulting in one death. 'There is a great need for improved dwellings, as well as sweeping away much of the existing insanitary property. No less than 100 houses have been found unfit for habitation and ought to be demolished. Many others will require extensive alteration and repair before being brought up to the standard now required for healthy living, and doubtless the adverse vital statistics of the borough is to a large extent due to this cause'. Until January 1919, refuse collection had been contracted out by the Corporation, but so many complaints had been received that the Corporation had decided to end the contract system and to purchase their own wagons and horses.[15] Now this particular wheel has turned full circle.

After all the tragedies of the war, the influenza epidemic was almost too much to have to bear:

'Influenza has wrought sad havoc in many homes in the county within the past few weeks. The list of losses is a mournful one, and includes a large number of men and women whom one might reasonably have supposed would survive attack by the robustness of their constitutions. The strong succumb as rapidly as the weak. There are distressing cases through whole families being down with the dread disease... . Probably the food supply has a near association with the progress of the disease in some cases. But there is no doubt that half the havoc caused is due to not taking especial care when the symptoms of the disease first appear, and to running risks when the crisis of the disease has passed. The after effects of influenza are often more disastrous than the disease itself'.[16]

Dr. Gregor was praised in the *Times* and the *British Medical Journal* for the work he had been carrying out for some years into the causes and prevention of influenza. Dr. Gregor had found that workers in a workroom in a factory in which the atmosphere was charged with a small amount of either nitrous oxide or sulphur dioxide gas enjoyed 'relative immunity' from influenza, whilst their fellow workers in other parts of the factory where there were no such gases 'were heavily attacked'. The Medical Research Committee was assisting Dr. Gregor in his research, and was commending his work to the Minister of Health, 'who no doubt is fully alive to the urgent need of a satisfactory method of preventing the spread of influenza'.[17]

The pitfalls of business were evidenced when a debtor in the local Bankruptcy Court showed a deficit of over £9000, having bought honey at £220 per ton, and sold it at £55 per ton. The *Packet* was not slow to point out that this lower figure 'is rather less than 6d per pound, and the present retail price of honey being 1s 9d to 2s per pound (the bees not having had a great increase in their pre-war wages), it seems that the burden is once more laid on the consumer'.[18]

The Corporation's proposal to pay for the official peace celebrations by levying a rate met with considerable public opposition, and it was agreed that the money should be raised by voluntary effort instead.[19] Once the peace treaty had been signed at Versailles, the 19th July was designated as the day on which the official celebrations should take place, and the town was bedecked with flags, bunting and other decorations. 'One of the finest processions ever seen in Falmouth' took place, incorporating the armed forces, veterans of the war and many civilian organisations. The streets were lined with people and a huge crowd assembled in the Moor, where a platform, prettily decorated with evergreens and bamboos, had been erected. Close to the platform was a German mine which had been picked up in Falmouth Bay and which has now been presented to the town by the naval authorities'. The Mayor (Mr. Spargo) addressed the crowd, paying tribute not only to the armed forces, the fallen and the veterans who had returned, but also to the civilian authorities, including the police - 'no less than 10,000 aliens passed through their hands and they made no mistake about them'. He also paid tribute to Mr. W.J.Walton, who acted as interpreter for and examination officer of aliens and 'who, by his shrewdness and great knowledge of foreign languages and detective ability was the means of bringing many Germans to book, men who tried to pass themselves off as Swedes, Danes or Russian Poles'. Later in the day, there was a children's fete, a carnival in the evening - 'mirth and jollity held sway for a few hours, and it is a source of pride that the unrestrained frivolity never overstepped the lines of decorum' - an open air concert, and a dance at Gyllyngdune Gardens, where a floor had been laid, ending with a fireworks display on the Hornwork. 'Looking towards the harbour, the sky was crossed in every direction by trails of coloured fire and sparks, and high above all were scores of splashes of brilliant red, blue, white and yellow stars'. Someone likened the Hornwork to an open stretch in Flanders under shell fire - hardly a happy memory for many there.[20]

The first summer of peace saw a renewal of trips on the *Queen of the Fal*. From Falmouth to Truro, return, cost 2s, to the Lizard, calling at Kynance and Coverack, 3s 6d, Mevagissey, Looe & Fowey, 3s 6d and Helford River, 2s.[21] After the privations of war, there was a rush to holiday in the south west, including Falmouth. On a Saturday in August, in order to accommodate passengers from Paddington, the Cornish Riviera consisted of 34 carriages hauled by three locomotives, and even then passengers were 'invited' to sit on the luggage in the guard's van.[22] Whilst this influx of visitors was good for the town's economy, and especially for the owners of hotels and guesthouses, there were those who worried whether the crowds would affect the town's popularity in future years, since in pre-war days 'people had come here for rest from the turmoil and crush of the outer world' and even in a resort like Falmouth 'there were comparatively few people in the streets and on the beaches - conducive to rest and a feeling of remoteness'. It was also alleged that scarcity of accommodation and food had encouraged profiteering - 'ridiculously high prices are often charged and complaints are numerous... Too many boarding house proprietors and shop keepers have forgotten the old adage, 'Don't kill the goose that lays the golden egg.''[23] A Mr. Browning of Staffordshire, wrote to the *Packet* claiming that his holiday in St. Mawes had been somewhat tarnished by the steep rise in prices for rooms in the past year. He went on, 'Now, sir, visitors have been hitherto prepared to put up with the insanitary and primitive conditions of St. Mawes, partly on account of its cheapness, but if the inhabitants are going to put up their prices they must be prepared to offer more up-to-date accommodation, some other system of refuse disposal than that of simply chucking it over the wall to foul the sea front must be adopted, water must be laid on and other conveniences supplied. In short, if they want the prices of fashionable watering places, they must offer the advantages of the same'.[24]

Falmouth was third in the sunshine stakes for the whole country in that summer, behind only Guernsey and Torquay.[25] There was a revival of the annual open tennis tournament in August, but the golf course was still occupied by the military, for which the Government paid the golf club £500 compensation.[26] That strict class distinctions were a fact of life despite the war is evidenced by a meeting of Falmouth Golf Club Company. 'In a place like Falmouth, there are class distinctions, and golfers liked to mix with their own set or class. Mr. Rickard suggested that they could have a club for the wealthy or leisured classes, one for the middle class and one for the artisans, all using the same course under properly drawn up regulations'.[27] The bowling club reported that its 12th season had been the most successful ever; they now had 54 members and the subscription was 15s 6d per annum. The Club had gained a renewal of its lease for another five years from the Recreation Ground Company, at a rent of £10 per annum.[28]

By the summer, the army had abandoned Trevethan camp, and a scheme for the purchase of the huts there for 'temporary dwellings for the working classes' had to be abandoned when all the buildings were sold by auction in November 1919. New houses were planned at Penwerris, the cost of building would be in the region of £670 a house.[29] Whilst all agreed that these were necessary, they brought with them their own problems. First among these was how they were to be subsidised; it had been calculated that a tenant would have to pay 13s a week in rent if there was no subsidy, but that the probable asking rent would be nearer 7s, so that between them the Government and the Corporation would have to subsidise the rent to the extent of 6s a week. Then the question arose as to who should have priority, those who had fought so bravely in the war or those living in the worst slum conditions, irrespective of whether they had fought or not. As the *Briton* put it, 'the problem is surrounded by many and peculiar difficulties'.[30] Comrades of the Great War, forerunner of the Royal British Legion, had 471 members in Falmouth by August 1919 and so were a powerful lobby, pressing for ex-servicemen to be given priority in housing and employment.[31] As work started on the construction of the 44 workmen's dwellings at Penwerris, concern was expressed that these houses would command rents beyond the pockets of working men, at £40 or £50 a year.[32] The lack of houses, particularly for men who had returned from the war and had married shortly after demobilisation, was a cause of considerable unrest, particularly when scarce building materials were used for the construction of leisure and sporting facilities. 'There is something rotten in the State when the men who fought cannot find houses for themselves, while amusements are lavishly catered for with the very materials required for houses'.[33]

Bureaucratic delay caused further anger:

'Government officials have accumulated thousands of tons of materials for housing, and thus reduced the supplies available for private builders. Meanwhile plans are being considered and reconsidered by officials whose distinctive attributes are slowness and smugness. Is it any wonder that men and women in want of houses get impatient and are ready to welcome any change that will end the prevailing paralysis?'[34]

The rehousing of war veterans was not by any means the only problem. The joy at the end of the slaughter was soon matched by exasperation at the slow demobilisation of those desperately needed in trades and businesses stretched to the limit. Contrasting the situation with the efficiency shown in getting men into khaki, the *Briton* stated, 'Now there is confusion, loss of time and general dissatisfaction... No sensible person wants or expects the preliminaries to demobilisation rushed. But people have the right to ask for business-like methods and that correspondence and form filling should be dealt with within a reasonable time... . If demobilisation is to go on smoothly, it must be in the hands of men who are acquainted with labour-saving office devices and methods and who are not interfered with and hampered at every turn by officials whose reputations were won in other spheres of usefulness'.[35]

The three largest steamers to be accommodated at the same time in dry dock at Falmouth were, in May 1919, the *Walmate*, 7,000 tons, refrigeration ship, the *Westmeath*, refrigeration ship, 9,000 tons, and the *Nirvana*, troop transport, 6,000 tons. The *Times* reported on the development of the docks, following the take-over of the docks company by Lord Inchcape's concern - [36] 'While gangs of men are engaged in repairing these ships, large numbers are busily employed on excavations for a new and much larger dry dock.Truly, there is a new spirit abroad in Falmouth. Her opportunities are realised, and an era of greater services to shipping - 'the jugular vein of the Empire' - and of increased prosperity to the inhabitants seems now to be opening'. The Chamber of Commerce did not quite share the *Times's* confident view of the future of the town; whilst pleasure was expressed at the number of men now employed at the docks, there was also concern at the lack of shipping since the end of the war. Members seemed to agree that what was needed was a new and up-to-date coaling station, which would capture the trade then enjoyed by Dartmouth. Mr. Chard thought that this could be done if local people would invest in their own town, 'but it seemed to him that certain local people with capital would much sooner invest in Mexican mines, Dutch undertakings, rubber estates or South African gold mines'.

The Chamber's caution over the prospective prosperity of the port seemed to be supported by the fact that in September 1919, Belgian liners, which had been calling regularly at Falmouth during the war, were diverted to Plymouth by the Home Office, because the Aliens' Officer had been moved from Falmouth to Plymouth. 'This is not only a typical example of red tape, but an unwarrantable interference with our freedom. It means that during the pleasure of those in authority in Whitehall, if not permanently, liners which happen to have aliens on board will be prohibited from using our harbour. What objection there can be to the Falmouth Customs officials now dealing with aliens as they used to do before the commencement of hostilities is difficult to imagine'. The *Packet* urged the Corporation and all public bodies in the town to take up the matter with the Home Office.[37]

The Chamber of Commerce was concerned with aspects of the town other than the port and docks. The chairman, Mr. Rusden, wanted to see an industrial factory to give employment to the female population, but Mr. Kestin said that this would not be a popular idea as, now the war was over, residents were looking for domestic servants, and a factory would diminish the number of women available for this. The question of advertising the town as a holiday resort arose, but it was pointed out that the town was already full of visitors and there was no accommodation for more. It was agreed that there was a need for a new hotel and that the town should be advertised as a winter holiday resort. The deplorable state of some boarding houses was alluded to.[38] A further concern was the increase in the general rate for Falmouth from 1s 9d in the £ to 2s 6d, 'and there are grave fears that even with a ninepenny advance sufficient money will be forthcoming to meet the expenditure... The situation looks most serious, and, unfortunately, there are no prospects of early relief, for fresh demands are being constantly made by Labour, and the cost of food and commodities is still soaring with the result that heavier taxation and rates must inevitably follow'.[39]

A national rail strike in October 1919 hit Cornwall hard, with all mines being closed down so as to conserve coal for pumping purposes, but it was settled after one week.[40] The Falmouth MP, Sir Edward Nicholl, served as an engine driver during the strike, having been an engineering apprentice with the Great Western in his youth.[41] There was considerable friction between Falmouth Unionist Club and Sir Edward, when the club refused to elect him as their president. The club had asked Sir Edward for a donation of £50, which he declined to make, saying that he had spent £3,500 in the constituency since his election, and that the preceding president had donated £5. Some correspondents to the *Packet* supported his attitude, but others bitterly criticised him, claiming that he had made his 'millions' in the war at the expense both of the workers and the fighting men. The *Briton* fully supported Sir Edward, stating that the Club 'must not expect overwhelming sympathy when they ask a president-designate to pay a fixed fee for the honour and shed their salt tears in public because the individual thus chosen for distinction places upon their offer a far different value'.[43] Sir Edward did not seem to be a particularly enthusiastic MP, but he had two main themes; the first was making Germany pay in full for the cost of the war, and the second was a fear of Bolshevism spreading to this country, particularly by Russian and European seamen landing in British ports.[44]

The Flushing War Memorial was dedicated in September 1919. Even a small village such as Flushing had sixteen names to inscribe on the memorial, eight naval and eight[45] military. A list of 212 names to be inscribed on the Falmouth War Memorial appeared in the Packet in January 1920, with a request that any omissions be notified to the committee.[46] The final number was 242, and a Memorial on Cliff Road was unveiled by the Lord Lieutenant, Mr. J.C. Williams, on the 24th May 1920, which recorded all these names, as did the War Memorial Tablet placed beneath the Memorial Window on the east wall of the Parish Church, which was unveiled in June 1924.[47] A ceremony was held on the Moor in September 1919, at which scrolls were presented to the families of those who had fallen. These scrolls were designed by Mr. L.A. Pownall and 'reproduced in many colours on Japanese vellum', and to which was affixed the seal of the Corporation and the signature of the Mayor. The latter, in his speech, struck a note of optimism - 'If the Great War has not broken down the barbed wire of caste and uprooted the social undergrowth of snobbishness, if it has not bound us together more closely by the common bond of suffering, if it has not given us a wider vision and a greater charity, if it has not opened our eyes to the miseries of those around us and kindled our hearts into action, then the lessons of the War have fallen on deaf ears. Our mission in life now is to fight for principles, to carry on a crusade against slums, to insist upon a healthier and a happier environment for those who have never had a chance to live a decent life, and to make our land a fit place for our returned heroes and their children to live in'.[48]

It has already been seen that the confidence over the future prosperity of the port as a result of the vast St. Just development scheme was beginning to wane in 1919, as doubts arose as to whether the finance would be available. The war had resulted in a high wage economy and full employment, but

Copy of a scroll presented by the Borough to all who had served in the war and to the next-of-kin of all who had died in the Service of their Country

now that this impetus was over, 'employers have to look to ordinary trade to supply the money for wages and other expenditure', and this would involve huge economies. In pre-war days, a great deal of coal was sold abroad, but in 1919 there was hardly enough for home needs. Many could see that the artificial war prosperity would be succeeded by prolonged and acute industrial distress.[49] The Levant mining disaster of October 1919 shocked the county. A relief fund was set up, and a dinner held at the Falmouth Hotel raised 1,000 guineas for this fund,[50] although it subsequently transpired that the bulk of this sum had been donated by guests from London at the dinner.[51]

The turn out of just over 50% for the municipal elections in November 1919 was considered disappointing. A Miss Whitburn became the first lady to be elected to the Council, winning the Smithick Ward.[52] The Falmouth Free Library Authority received a request that among the papers in the reading room should be the *Daily Herald*, which strongly supported the Labour Party. The Authority, albeit not unanimously, decided against this on the grounds that the *Herald* 'had not shown the spirit of patriotism which it ought to have shown' and there were dark hints that it was funded from outside the country.[53]

A total of £164,395 was raised in Falmouth in subscriptions to the Victory Loan bonds.[54] Since the outbreak of war, over £600,000 had been raised in Falmouth for War and Victory Loans. Special campaign weeks such as Gun Week, Aeroplane Week, Munitions Week were organised and one of these weeks raised £166,000, which was nearly £13 for each head of the population.[55] A tank had been presented to the town in recognition of its efforts in raising these funds, but by November 1919, 'it stands (on the Moor) a forlorn relic of the Great War, a plaything for the children to romp over and a dumping place for all the loose stones and debris that can, by any juvenile ingenuity, be deposited in its interior'.[56] Six years later, the tank was still there, and the Chamber of Commerce suggested that the tank should be sold for scrap as 'a nuisance and an eye sore', but were told that the tank did not belong to the Council, which was therefore unable to remove it. Quite to whom it

Arrival in Falmouth of a tank presented to the town, it was put on display to the west of the Packet Memorial

did belong was not made clear.[57] Other mementoes presented to the town were a field gun, which for some years was placed on Castle Drive, and a mine swept up in Falmouth Bay, which had its place in the Municipal Buildings.

A study by Sir T.H. Middleton of the Board of Agriculture of a comparison between the productivity of German and British farmers caused considerable controversy, as the report showed that in the production of corn, potatoes, meat, milk and sugar, the German farmer was by far the more productive. The reasons put forward for this had nothing to do with the German farmer being better at his job - perish the thought. Middleton suggested that it was due to improved technical and business methods, to profits being ploughed back into the business, and the use by German small farmers of cooperatives, enabling them to buy and sell as advantageously as their bigger brethren.[58]

The Mission to Seamen had been very busy in Falmouth. During 1918, 1,027 visits were made to HM ships, 1,840 to merchant ships, 230 to quay or dock and 94 to hospitals. The local chaplain described the average seaman as 'fine in physique, magnificent in courage, splendid in devotion to duty, but by reason of his calling, he was so long away from grace that there was a moral weakness that came upon him through the nature and character of his work'.[59] 'Moral weakness' was also concerning the Falmouth Trades Council, who were considering holding a masked ball, but one of their members thought that by advocating dances, the Council 'were helping their lads on to ruin.... . Dancing was a curse to young men, and it seemed to be encouraged by ministers and all the leaders of the various chapels'.[60]

A summary of the year 1919 in Falmouth appeared in the *Western Morning News*, painting a picture of considerable optimism and prosperity:

'In the summer the district maintained its popularity as a health and pleasure resort, the number of visitors constituting a record. Important extensions, and the construction of a new dry dock, have been in progress at the docks, and the foundry has worked at full pressure. The American Shipping Board have decided to make Falmouth their headquarters for repairs of their vessels on this side of the Atlantic. The old Ponsharden shipbuilding yard between Penryn and Falmouth has been taken over by the Exe-Transport Co., who have reconstructed it, deepened the dock and erected workshops, and it is now quite a busy spot, with over 150 men employed. Progress has also been made recently in the establishing of coal and oil stations in the harbour for shipping'.[61]

Agreement had been reached with the Great Western Railway for the advertising of Falmouth as a holiday resort, on the same terms as pre-war, and, although some doubts were expressed as to whether Falmouth could be developed both as a shipping and commercial centre and a holiday resort, the general view was that this was perfectly possible as the development of the harbour and the consequent increase in shipping would be an added attraction to holiday makers.[62] A large firm of net makers was looking for existing premises in Falmouth for a factory intended to employ 1,000 female workers, the cost of building new premises being prohibitive, but nothing of the appropriate size was available.[63] 'A Visitor' wrote to the *Packet* saying that, as an invalid, he had greatly benefited from a month's stay in Falmouth as a result of the sea air and warm climate, and intended to prolong his stay, but, now that he was getting better, he found that 'there is a decided dearth of amusement', the lighting in the town was very poor and the main street and pavement narrow and susceptible to accidents. He suggested the provision of a winter garden with good music and a skating rink attached, and one should be able to get warm sea water baths'.[64]

Whilst at the end of 1919, optimism for the future of Falmouth was apparent, one can still sense the underlying unease. The town had experienced four years of being of national importance, and had been indeed 'the principal war zone of the county',[65] combining an important naval base with a large army garrison and training area. In addition its geographical position highlighted its vital importance to the merchant marine of all nations bringing supplies to the United Kingdom in time of war. The huge influx of service personnel must have offset by far any economic loss in the holiday industry, but even the latter had benefited from the fact that the wealthy could no longer take their holidays on the continent, and from the loss of custom suffered by the east coast resorts as the result of Zeppelin and enemy warship raids. Falmouth had suffered, as all towns had suffered, from the loss and crippling of so many of their young men, and grief and sadness was everywhere, but its prestige and importance to the nation had never been greater. With great developments in the docks, the prospect of a huge new port at St. Just and an enhanced reputation as a holiday resort, what was there to stop the growing prosperity, and indeed the growing population?

And yet, and yet... There were those, the *Briton* amongst them, who saw that the country had neared bankruptcy in financing the war, that the boost that the war had given to the economy and to employment could not last once peace was restored, and, above all, that it was the conditions of war that had made Falmouth vital to the needs of the country. As soon as the war ended, the dream that the Admiralty would make a long term investment in Falmouth ended as well. Suddenly, public money was again at a premium, and the Navy had a perfectly good south western base at Plymouth, so why invest in Falmouth which only became important in time of war, which it was sincerely hoped would never occur again? The same argument applied to the merchant shipping of all nations. Falmouth was most useful when mines and submarines made voyaging further up the Channel dangerous, but once this danger was removed, it was economically advantageous to use the better communications of southern ports such as Southampton, and much more convenient for liner passengers. The ugly fact, from Falmouth's angle, was that its competitors had their facilities in place, whilst those of Falmouth were mainly on the drawing board. The hard headed financiers soon saw that even if the St. Just scheme went ahead, there was no certainty, or indeed really compelling reason, that the shipping companies would want to switch their custom to Falmouth. Without the new port, the associated industries would not come and there would be no new rail link. St. Just, therefore, was left to be a place of peace and pleasure for generations to come. Putting aside the agonies of war, Falmouth had enjoyed a peak of importance and prosperity, which could not be sustained when peace was restored. Its future was not to be so different from its pre-war past; a lovely place to have a holiday, ensuring a tourist industry in good times and bad, coupled with a busy port specialising in ship repairing. But for four years, 'Falmouth for instructions' had reverberated around the world.

NOTES

[1] FP, 24.1.1919, p2
[2] FP, 7.3.1919, p6
[3] FP, 11.1.1919, p3
[4] FP, 7.2.1919, p3
[5] FP, 28.3.1919, p3
[6] FP, 21.2.1919
[7] FP, 7.3.1919, p5
[8] FP, 21.3.1919, p4
[9] FP, 14.11.1919, p5
[10] WB, 15.5.1919, p2
[11] WB, 18.9.1919, p6
[12] FP, 16.5.1919, p5
[13] FP, 16.5.1919, p5
[14] FP, 15.8.1919, p5
[15] FP, 16.5.1919, p3
[16] WB, 3.3.1919, p2
[17] *The Times*, 4.11.1919, and the *BMJ*, as reprinted in FP, 7.11.1919, p5
[18] FP, 4.7.1919, p5
[19] FP, 16.5.1919, p5
[20] FP, 25.7.1919, p3
[21] FP, 1.8.1919, p1

[22] FP, 15.8.1919
[23] WB, 18.8.1919, p2
[24] FP, 8.8.1919, p6
[25] FP, 29.8.1919, p4
[26] WB, 23.5.1918, p7
[27] FP, 5.9.1919, p5
[28] WB, 30.10.1919, p5
[29] FP, 15.8.1919, p5
[30] WB, 2.12.1918, p2
[31] FP, 29.8.1919, p4
[32] FP, 17.10.1919, p3
[33] WB, 1.9.1919, p2
[34] WB, 15.9.1919, p2
[35] WB, 13.1.1919, p2
[36] *The Times*, 23.5.1919, reprinted in FP, 30.5.1919, p3
[37] FP, 12.9.1919, p5
[38] FP, 22.8.1919, p4
[39] FP, 12.9.1919, p5
[40] FP, 3.10.1919, p3
[41] FP, 10.10.1919, p6
[42] FP, 29.11.1919, p3
[43] WB, 4.12.1919

[44] WB, 3.4.1919, p7
[45] FP, 3.10.1919, p3
[46] FP, 30.1.1920, p2
[47] W. Lloyd Fox, ibid.
[48] FP, 26.9.1919, p3
[49] WB, 25.8.1919, p2
[50] FP, 7.11.1919, p4
[51] FP, 7.11.1919, p4
[52] FP, 7.11.1919, p5
[53] FP, 22.8.1919, p2
[54] FP, 18.7.1919, p5
[55] Wilson Lloyd Fox, ibid.
[56] FP, 14.11.1919, p5
[57] FP, 23.4.1926
[58] WB, 30.10.1919, p2
[59] WB, 27.11.1919
[60] WB, 15.12.1919
[61] WMN, reprinted in FP, 9.1.1920, p4
[62] FP, 21.11.1919, p5
[63] FP, 21.11.1919, p5
[64] FP, 12.12.1919, p7
[65] WMN, 29.12.1918

APPENDIX

Extracts from a letter from Corporal Robert T. Stephens, with the British forces fighting in Mesopotamia, to his father, Mr. J. Gilbert Stephens, JP, of 'Ashfield', Falmouth, July 1915, which has resonances for 2004. The two gaps were deletions by the military censor.

When I last wrote we were staying down at ...., but have since moved to our present position near the firing line. The river journey takes nearly .... to come up here although it is only about two hundred miles, the travelling being very slow owing to the swift current and having to tie up to the bank at night.

The Tigris is a fine river, but navigation is very difficult owing to the shifting mud banks and the very sharp corners; the river winds to such an extent that sometimes you find it almost retracing its steps. If it was not for the intense discomfort of being crowded on the limited space of a small paddle boat the trip would be quite enjoyable; as it was the experience was unique. Imagine the old tub snorting along with the cumbrous lighters on either side, each with an Arab pilot wielding a long pole on the bows to find out the mud banks! In places the current must run six or seven miles an hour, and it often takes an hour to get round a bend less than a mile long. When the bends are very sharp they employ the useful method of bumping against the bank, which, with a tremendous shock, throws the bows across the stream, enabling them to get round. Frequently you run onto the mud, and then have to go astern and wobble off sideways.

Little naked Arab children follow you for miles along the bank, sometimes wading in the mud and swimming out for biscuits thrown to them. At other times you pass an Arab encampment, and the whole population turns out with their arms full of screaming chicken and baskets of eggs, and try to strike bargains as you go along. At night, when tied up to the bank, you must have a strong guard on or you will find that the same people will raid you and cut your throats! The Arab here is very treacherous and distinctly hostile, and if you come across one when alone, away from the camp, well, if you don't, he will!

The heat up here is terrific. We have had about 116 degrees in the shade, and it is generally about 110 degrees. The minimum is high too, about 85 to 90 degrees as a rule, so the nights are not very refreshing. It is not as trying as down river, because the heat is dryer here. To you at home, a shade temperature like that must seem terrific, but really you get quite used to it and don't notice it much. As an illustration, sometimes a piece of iron in the shade is too hot to touch!

The Persian hills stand up in the distance about forty miles away, I should think, and do not look at all inviting. The good old Tigris is our best friend here, and a plunge off the bank every evening does worlds to freshen you up and keep you fit, in fact it's the one enjoyable hour of the day, and the water is fairly cool too, which makes it very refreshing.

You can buy practically nothing here except occasionally a tin or two of milk, which you can pay a rupee or more for. Very rarely you can get a tin of fruit on the steamers, for the exorbitant price of two rupees or more, so you see we are not very civilised here.

This country is simply crawling with all kinds of strange insects and reptiles. First and foremost come the locusts, which are like large grasshoppers, only they can fly, and their chief aim seems to be to come and keep you company in the tents. Then at night, of course, our friends the mosquitoes get busy, but up here they are not as bad as down the river. Beetles of all sorts are everywhere, some of them with bodies as large as an egg. There is also a kind of land crab which runs at a tremendous pace. Last night I woke up and found one inside my mosquito net, but promptly chased him out. There are a few tarantulas - a sort of large spider which bites you and which, I believe, is very dangerous - but I have seen only a few, fortunately. We get a lot of hyenas round the camps at night, making most weird cries. At first you think the sound is a human being shrieking, it is just like it; and last, but not least, Arabs sometimes think fit to wander round at night after horses and rifles - they are so wily that they will even rob a tent with men sleeping in it.[1]

There are many descriptions of life in the trenches for the infantrymen. We know less what it was like to be a gunner. The following graphic description of a night on the Italian front was sent by a gunner, Sergeant Rex H. Cox, son of Mr. and Mrs. Harold Cox, of Falmouth to the *Packet*.

'The day had been very hot and thundery, and since early morning the high plateau had been hidden by driving rain. Lightning, vivid and clean cut, had flashed and glittered upon the hills while the heavy roll and boom of the thunder had added its quota to the never ceasing rumble of the guns. At length, however, the grey, dull skies showed a line of brilliant blue low down upon the horizon which gradually broadened and deepened until the sun, though invisible to us, sent a ray of rain washed sunlight down upon the slate coloured waters of the Adriatic. The day was drawing to a close and it was already dusk, though, as the clouds were slowly driven away, the light increased until at length the sapphire dome of the sky, lightened in the west by the last rays of the sun, was entirely clear of any sign of the artillery duel of nature which had been in progress during the day. If the skies now showed no traces of the storm, not so the earth. Every trench was still a rushing torrent, every gunpit a quagmire, with the gun wheels sinking slowly in the clinging mud. Every man in the Battery was soaked to the skin and covered in mud from boot soles to eyebrows; the roads were deep in slush into which the thick dust turned at the slightest shower, and lorries and motor bikes skidded and slid, endangering their drivers and upsetting the usual orderly flow of traffic.

Back in the Battery, things were gradually settling down for the night, the rate of fire had slackened; supper, such as it was, had finished, and the men were preparing to get what sleep they could in the rock-blasted dug-outs, damp and clammy, and with water continually dropping from their roofs. A sudden call of 'night line' from the officer on duty in the Battery, brought the No.1 of each gun (two sergeants and two corporals) at the double to the small covered-in bay in the side of a trench which served the battery commander as a sleeping and working room. The night line was given out to each No.1, who put it in his note book, to prevent any error. Then came the tussle to get the guns out of the deep ruts into which they had sunk, and to haul them up so that they could be trained onto the new line. The weary gun teams heaved and strained upon the drag ropes, each gun seeming to resist as though it, too, was tired, and only wished to be left alone. At last the wheels and trail were clear, and the former were slowly carried round until the faint light of the lamp on the picket, which served as an aiming point for the layers during night firing, came into the field of view of the sight. 'Take post', and the trail was dropped; a turn or two of the traversing gear and the gun was laid.

A shell, ready fused, was brought up in the bearer and laid upon the trail, ready for instant action. Then the tired, rain soaked figures of the gun teams dragged their mud laden boots into the comparative warmth and dryness of the gun pit dug-outs, and dropped in all kinds of attitudes and tried to sleep. An armed sentry was posted at each gun, one detachment supplying the whole guard, being relieved at the end of its period of duty by the next, and so on through the night. It was now quite dark, with a thin slip of moon low down on the horizon and countless stars shining clear and bright in the cloudless sky. Away up in front of the guns were the four yellow specks of light from the picket lamps, while down in the valley a few glimmers of light could be seen, reflections from the interiors of Italian dug-outs and billets. The dark, muffled figures of the sentries, with rifles slung Italian fashion, muzzles up, from the right shoulder, showed up occasionally against the sky line in clear cut silhouette, as they tramped to and fro, striving to overcome the ever growing chill from their rain soaked uniforms. In No.2 gun pit dug-out a faint light showed where the No.1, who was in charge of the guard, was writing home. A guttering, flickering candle served him for illumination, and occasionally he would heave himself to his feet and come into the open. A few steps brought him to the next gun. 'Everything OK?' 'Yes, sergeant.' 'Right'; and so on to the next, until all had been visited. Then, returning to his dug-out he would cast a glance towards the ridge to see if all the picket lamps were burning, listen to the intermittent gun fire, and watch the flashes from the surrounding hills. Nothing, however, was unusual, and he was turning to enter the dug-out, when a long drawn whine signified the coming of an enemy shell. The whine increased to a scream, and the scream to a whistling rush, as the shell, a high velocity medium calibre, from the sound, passed close overhead and burst in the valley behind with a crash that echoed and re-echoed from hill to hill.

As the echoes died away the patter of the falling rock and steel fragments could be heard, whilst a larger piece whirred away like some monster bee. Right on the heels of the first came another, bursting shorter on the side of the hill just in rear of the battery; five or six more came over in rapid succession, the last bursting in front of and close to No.1 gun, causing the NCO and the sentries to duck quickly under the shelter of the low sandbag walls of the gun pits, whilst the jagged pieces hissed and screamed past, some hitting the rocky surface with a 'Ping-g-g' and ricochetting away into the darkness. As suddenly as it commenced, the firing ceased; the target had evidently been the road which passed along the valley and which during the night was crowded with traffic of all descriptions, motor lorries, ammunition limbers, ambulance vans and long lines of infantry in single file on either side, on their way up to, and back from, the front line trenches. As though the sudden burst of fire had been a signal, a brilliant, blinding glare filled the valley as the white searching rays of a giant enemy searchlight probed and searched for any movement. The rumble of traffic stopped, except at those places in the road, which, by reason of bends in the valley line, lay in deep shadow. The camouflage screens which were erected by the side of the roads visible from the enemy's lines, stood out clear and strong in the white glare. The searchlight lay along the valley like a solid mass for ten minutes and then swept up the side of the hill and was cut off by the high ground in front. Then came the sharp punching reports of a Battery of 75s on the other side of the ridge, the almost invariable accompaniment to a visit of the huge light to this part of the line, and the shells went screaming away towards that great white eye, which, steady and menacing, flared across from the heights behind the enemy's lines. Although many hundreds of rounds have been hurled across to smash that light which haughtily and calmly shone on as though nothing could disturb it, yet it has never been hit. There was nothing wrong with the shooting, but the light was so well hidden and protected that no falling shell could damage it. Suddenly, as though a curtain had been drawn, the light went out, and the eyes were almost dazzled by the ensuing darkness.

All was quiet again, save for a fitful gun fire which was so much a matter of course that it was hardly noticed, but not for long - a sudden chatter of machine gun fire, scattered volleys of rifle fire and close upon them, the sharp reports of field artillery, told that something unusual was occurring. The whip-like cracks of field guns and 75s up in front increased in volume and intensity, the sharp, stabbing flashes piercing the darkness with gashes of yellow flame, while white and red Verey lights soared upwards and hung over the trenches. The night was full of sound and the sentries stood by for the 'alarm'. The telephonist on duty jumped to his feet, with a message from Group HQ in his hand and raced along the trench to the dug-out of the officer on duty. Almost at once the short, sharp blasts of 'action' from this officer's whistle cut into the inferno of noise, like a locomotive's whistle in a tunnel. The sentry at each gun dived into the gun dug-out and woke the detachments; still half dazed with sleep they turn out and each No.1 prepares to receive his orders. They are not long in coming. The shells are lifted, slid into the chambers and with swinging lunges of the rammers, the copper bands are driven home into the riflings with ringing 'plunks'. The shadowy muzzles are slowly lifted, the No.1s flash their electric torches over the sights and check the lay; Nos.2 hook their lanyards and stand clear, and the silent death dealers are ready. The officer picks up his megaphone: -'Battery, Fire!!' Shadowy forms turn sharply to the right, lanyards tighten and the firing pins are pulled clear. The darkness is cleft by four vivid, blinding flashes, and the reverberating reports of howitzers firing together shakes the air and brings the dry camouflage spinning down upon the guns and their teams. The muzzles drop and breeches are opened; thin films of smoke filter away into the air and more shells are driven home.

And so it goes on; the weary gun teams working mechanically; the two men fusing shells beside the gun pit almost working in their sleep. One can imagine them thinking, 'Why can't they let us rest?' But they go on, every NCO and man doing his work quickly and correctly, although hardly conscious of what he does, and yet from the habit of long practice, nothing is done wrong.

In the early hours of the morning, the rate of fire slackens and the men become more conscious of what is going on around them. The inferno of noise in front has lessened and the machine gun and rifle fire can be heard between the bursts of gun fire. The enemy's counter-attack has failed, and he is drawing back his troops, those that remain, through a barrage of shrapnel and high explosive to his own lines. At length comes the welcome order, 'Cease Fire'. The hot, reeking guns are then sponged out, new sentries are posted and the men almost dropping from fatigue, with parched throats and smarting eyes, eyelashes and eyebrows singed and faces blackened by the back-flash, stumble wearily to their blankets and once more fall asleep.

The floors of the gun-pits are by now a mass of churned mud into which the feet sink until boots are out of sight; the trail has sunk far below its normal depth and the gun wheels are half way to the axles. Then the enemy, according to his custom, begins, and shells begin to scream over and around; a barrage of shrapnel and HE sweeps the roads and hill sides and the air is full of the whine and scream of fragments and the shattering crashes of bursts. But already most of the men are asleep; and the bombardment does not waken them for theirs is the deep sleep of utter exhaustion. Hard, heavy toil in a trying climate, night after night of broken rest and furious activity, tell on the hardiest, and nature must be appeased. So they sleep for a few short hours, forgetful of all hardships, and perchance carried in spirit to the Homeland where lie, safe and undisturbed, those they love best'.[2]

NOTES

[1] Reprinted in FP, 4.8.1916, p5

[2] FP, 25.1.1918, p3

BIBLIOGRAPHY

Cornwall Studies Centre, Redruth

Newspapers:
The Falmouth Packet
The West Briton

Royal Cornwall Polytechnic Society, Falmouth

Unpublished Manuscripts:
Wilson Lloyd Fox, 'Falmouth and the Great War', Presidential address to the Royal Cornwall Polytechnic Society, undated, but possibly 1924

Mrs Faith Harris, 'A Falmouth Lady's Diary, 1914-1917'

J.J. Lawrie, 'The Story of the *Mary B. Mitchell'*, Carrickfergus & District Historical Journal, volume 8, 1995, pp6-16

J. Manley, 'Log of H.M.S. *Mary B. Mitchell*' , undated.

E.J. Moseley, 'Mine and Anti-Submarine Operations Carried Out During The War, off the Cornish Coast', undated.

Published Articles:
Arthur Marwick, 'British Life & Leisure In The First World War', *History Today*, June 1965

Books:
John Bickersteth, editor, *The Bickersteth Diaries, 1914-1918*, Leo Cooper, 1998

Vera Brittain, *Testament of Youth*, Virago, 1980

E. Keble Chatterton, *Beating The U-boats*, Hurst & Blackett, London, 1943

Bob Dunstan, *The Book of Falmouth & Penryn*, 1975

Richard Van Emden & Steve Humphries, *All Quiet On The Home Front*, Headline Book Publishing, 2003

J.D. Grainger, editor, *The Maritime Blockade of Germany in the Great War*, Navy Records Society, 2003

Nicholas Lambert, editor, *The Submarine Service, 1900-1918*, Navy Records Society, 2001

Robert K. Massie, *Castles of Steel*, Jonathan Cape, 2004

E. Sylvia Pankhurst, *The Home Front*, Hutchinson & Co., London, 1932

Mr. Punch's History of the Great War, Cassell & Co., London, 1920

A.J.P. Taylor, *The First World War*, Penguin Books, 1966

Bernard Walk, *Twenty Years at St. Hilary*, Truran, 2002

James Whetter, *The History of Falmouth*, Dyllansow Truran, Redruth, 1981